A Guide to Global

**Offshore Outsourcing and
Other Global Delivery Models**

The British Computer Society

The British Computer Society is the leading professional body for the IT industry. With members in over 100 countries, the BCS is the professional and learned Society in the field of computers and information systems.

The BCS is responsible for setting standards for the IT profession. It is also leading the change in public perception and appreciation of the economic and social importance of professionally managed IT projects and programmes. In this capacity, the Society advises, informs and persuades industry and government on successful IT implementation.

IT is affecting every part of our lives and that is why the BCS is determined to promote IT as *the* profession of the 21st century.

Joining the BCS

BCS qualifications, products and services are designed with your career plans in mind. We not only provide essential recognition through professional qualifications but also offer many other useful benefits to our members at every level.

Membership of the BCS demonstrates your commitment to professional development. It helps to set you apart from other IT practitioners and provides industry recognition of your skills and experience. Employers and customers increasingly require proof of professional qualifications and competence. Professional membership confirms your competence and integrity and sets an independent standard that people can trust. www.bcs.org/membership

Further Information

Further information about the British Computer Society can be obtained from: The British Computer Society, 1 Sanford Street, Swindon, Wiltshire, SN1 1HJ.

Telephone: +44 (0)1793 417 424
Email: bcs@hq.bcs.org.uk
Web: www.bcs.org

A Guide to Global Sourcing

Offshore Outsourcing and Other Global Delivery Models

Elizabeth Anne Sparrow

THE BRITISH COMPUTER SOCIETY

© 2005 The British Computer Society

All rights reserved. Apart from any fair dealing for the purposes of research or private study, or criticism or review, as permitted by the Copyright Designs and Patents Act 1988, no part of this publication may be reproduced, stored or transmitted in any form or by any means, except with the prior permission in writing of the Publisher, or in the case of reprographic reproduction, in accordance with the terms of the licences issued by the Copyright Licensing Agency. Enquiries for permission to reproduce material outside those terms should be directed to the Publisher.

The British Computer Society,
1 Sanford Street,
Swindon, Wiltshire SN1 1HJ,
UK
www.bcs.org

ISBN 1-902505-61-1

British Cataloguing in Publication Data.
A CIP catalogue record for this book is available at the British Library.

All trademarks, registered names etc acknowledged in this publication are to be the property of their respective owners.

Disclaimer:
Although every care has been taken by the authors and The British Computer Society in the preparation of the publication, no warranty is given by the authors or The British Computer Society as Publisher as to the accuracy or completeness of the information contained within it and neither the authors nor The British Computer Society shall be responsible or liable for any loss or damage whatsoever arising by virtue of such information or any instructions or advice contained within this publication or by any of the aforementioned.

Typeset by Tradespools, Frome, Somerset.
Printed at Antony Rowe Ltd.

Contents

List of figures and tables	vii
Author	viii
Foreword Martyn Hart	ix
Acknowledgements	x
Abbreviations	xi
Glossary	xiii
Useful websites	xiv
Preface Elizabeth Sparrow	xvi

1 Introduction — 1
  The origins and growth of the offshore market — 4
  Business models — 6
  Work permits — 12
  Responses to the offshore outsourcing trend — 13

2 Advantages and benefits — 25
  Cost reduction — 25
  Other economic advantages — 27
  Quality management — 28
  Follow the sun — 34
  Access to skills and resources — 35
  Greater focus on core business objectives — 36
  Productivity and service improvements — 37
  Business transformation and new developments — 38

3 Risks and countermeasures — 39
  Hidden costs — 40
  Cultural differences — 40
  Geopolitical instability and difficult business environments — 43
  Legal issues – including intellectual property protection — 44
  Security, confidentiality and data protection — 46
  Loss of technical expertise and business knowledge — 49
  Loss of flexibility and control — 50
  Customer backlash — 52
  Negative impact on IT professionals — 53

4	Managing offshore outsourcing projects	57
	Sourcing strategy	59
	Identifying what to source offshore	62
	Objectives	64
	Statement of requirements	67
	Investigating the IT services market	68
	Choosing a service provider	69
	Outsourcing contracts	76
	Transition	82
	Managing performance	83
5	Country profiles	89
	General information resources	91
	Key to country profiles	96
	Brazil	97
	Bulgaria	99
	Canada	102
	China	104
	The Czech Republic	108
	Hungary	110
	India	112
	Ireland	122
	Israel	125
	Malaysia	127
	Mexico	129
	The Philippines	131
	Poland	135
	Romania	137
	Russia	140
	Singapore	143
	South Africa	146
	Vietnam	149
6	The future world of global sourcing	153
	Appendix Intellect Offshore Group Code of Practice	157
	References	159
	Further reading	160
	Index	163

List of Figures and Tables

Figure 4.1 Nine steps to successful offshore outsourcing
Figure 4.2 Sourcing strategy
Figure 4.3 Evaluation
Figure 4.4 Successful outsourcing relationships
Table 1.1 Global delivery models
Table 2.1 Advantages of offshore sourcing
Table 2.2 CMM levels
Table 2.3 The virtual helpdesk
Table 3.1 Offshore sourcing risks
Table 4.1 Advantages and disadvantages of single- or multi-sourcing

Author

Elizabeth Sparrow is an author and consultant, specializing in outsourcing relationships and change management programmes. Prior to her freelance career, Elizabeth was a senior IT leader in the public sector and worked with many different outsourcing service providers. As IT Director at the Home Office she led a major infrastructure upgrade project and launched an innovative private finance initiative. While at the Crown Prosecution Service, Elizabeth coordinated a substantial change programme involving not only the Crown Prosecution Service, but also the police and courts. Elizabeth's first book Successful IT Outsourcing was published in 2003.

Foreword

Elizabeth Sparrow and I have worked together in the Home Office, both running different major outsourcing programmes that were leading edge at their time. So I can vouch for her expertise in the subject area, her thoroughness at tackling the problems faced and for the success of the programmes she led.

Elizabeth has constructed an unusually helpful guide to offshore outsourcing here, not just suggesting the processes that you should go through, but very cleverly linking to many authentic case studies demonstrating how actual organizations have tackled the problems in real life. Also she forewarns the reader of potential problems and explains how you can take steps to mitigate them.

Offshore outsourcing IT systems can bring immense benefits if managed correctly, and one of the most important aspects of this management is planning. With this book, Elizabeth gives you not just the road map for the way ahead, but unlike most maps, she tells you where the roadworks might be and how to get around them!

Martyn Hart
Chair of the European Outsourcing Association
Amsterdam
June 2004
www.e-oa.net

Acknowledgements

Many people have helped enlighten me in this new world of global sourcing. My special thanks for their contributions to this book go to Martyn Hart, Mark Kobayashi-Hillary, Alan Hopwood, Rosie Symons, Roger Baker, Rachel Burnett, Nick Kalisperas and Richard Sykes at Intellect, Ian Durrant at the Professional Contractors' Group, Matthew Dixon, Ian Conway at i-Vantage, Sunil Masra at Mastek and Prabhuu Sinha at Satyam Computer Services

My friends at the British Computer Society have encouraged and supported me through the production of this book – thank you to Sue McNaughton, Suzanna Marsh and Elaine Boyes. A word of thanks also to my reviewers who offered such helpful feedback.

And finally my thanks go to my husband Alan Gurney who has as ever helped in all sorts of ways.

Abbreviations

ABES	Brazilian Association of Software Companies
AMITI	Mexican Association of the Information Technology Industry
ANIS	National Association of the Software Industry and Services (Romania)
APKIT	Information and Computer Technologies Industry Association (Russia)
ARIES	Romanian Association for the Electronic and Software Industry
ASSESPRO	Association of the Brazilian Companies of Software and IT Services
ATIC	Romanian Association for Information Technology and Communications
BAIT	Bulgarian Association of Information Technologies
BJP	Bharatiya Janata Party (India)
CBI	Confederation of British Industry
CC	Common Criteria security accreditation scheme
CISSP	Certified Information System Security Professional
CMM	Capability Maturity Model
CMMI	Capability Maturity Model Integration
CSIA	China Software Industry Association
CWU	Communication Workers' Union
DMAIC	Define, Measure and Analyse, Improve and Control
DPMO	Defects per Million Opportunities
DSSS	Development of Six Sigma Software
DTI	Department of Trade and Industry (UK)
EEA	European Economic Area
EIU	Economist Intelligence Unit
EU	European Union
FTE	Full Time Equivalent
GDP	Gross Domestic Product
HKITF	Hong Kong Information Technology Federation
HSA	Hungarian Software Alliance
IASH	Israeli Association of Software Houses
IBG	India Business Group
ICT	Information and Communication Technologies
IMF	International Monetary Fund
ISA	Irish Software Association
ISO	International Standards Organization

ISP	Internet Service Provider
ITAP	Information Technology Association of the Philippines
IVSZ	Hungarian Association of Information Technology Companies
ITAA	Information Technology Association of America
ITAC	Information Technology Association of Canada
ITIL	Information Technology Infrastructure Library
ITSEC	IT Security Evaluation Criteria
KPI	Key Performance Indicator
MII	Ministry of Information Industry (China)
NAFTA	North America Free Trade Act
NASSCOM	National Association of Software and Services Companies (India)
NATO	North Atlantic Treaty Organization
NOA	National Outsourcing Association (UK)
OECD	Organisation for Economic Co-operation and Development
OJEC	Official Journal of the European Community
PCG	Professional Contractors' Group
P-CMM	People Capability Maturity Model
PIIT	Polish Chamber of Information Technology and Telecommunications
PIKOM	Association of the Computer and Multimedia Industry, Malaysia
RFI	Request for Information
RFP	Request for Proposals
RUSSOFT	National Software Development Association of Russia
SA-CMM	Software Acquisition Capability Maturity Model
SE-CMM	System Engineering Capability Maturity Model
SEI	Carnegie Mellon University's Software Engineering Institute
SiTF	Singapore infocomm Technology Federation
SSE-CMM	System Security Engineering Capability Maturity Model
STPI	Software Technology Parks of India
Sucesu-SP	Society for IT and Telecommunications Users – Sao Paulo
SW-CMM	Capability Maturity Model for Software
T-CMM	Trusted Capability Maturity Model
TCS	Tata Consultancy Services
TfL	Transport for London
TRIPS	Trade-Related aspects of Intellectual Property rightS
TSP	Team Software Process
TUPE	Transfer of Undertakings (Protection of Employment) Regulations
UPA	United Progressive Alliance (India)
VINASA	Vietnam Software Association
WIPO	World Intellectual Property Organization
WITSA	World Information Technology and Services Alliance

Glossary

In this rapidly developing field, terminology is still evolving. The following definitions have been adopted within this book:

Outsourcing The transfer of responsibility for any IT service, including planning, management and operations, to an external service provider.

Offshore outsourcing The transfer of responsibility for any IT service, but especially application development, to an external service provider based in another country. Offshore outsourcing can be divided into:

> **Near-shore outsourcing** The use of services provided by a nearby country.
>
> **Far-shore outsourcing** The use of services provided by countries further away.
>
> There are no hard and fast rules defining which countries would be considered as 'near' and which would be treated as 'far'.

Inshore or home-shore outsourcing The transfer of responsibility for IT services to an external service provider employing local staff and based in the same country as the client.

Onshore outsourcing IT services are provided by staff from an outsourcing company who may employ local staff, or may provide overseas employees who work in the client organization's own country under work permit or visa arrangements. These staff may work on the client's site or at a remote office, but still within the same country as the client.

Offshoring An abbreviation for offshore sourcing.

Backsourcing The process of re-establishing an IT function to take responsibility for services that have previously been outsourced.

Business process outsourcing The transfer of responsibility for the planning, management and operation of an entire business process (including any supporting IT systems) to an external service provider.

Insourcing The formal adoption of the internal IT department as service provider, governed by a service level agreement against which performance is monitored.

Useful Websites

These sites offer general information about offshore outsourcing, advice and guidance, papers, information about forthcoming events, offshore supplier information and news articles.

Computerworld Knowledge Center The Offshore Buyer's guide includes general advice and guidance as well as articles about the IT services industry in a number of countries:
www.computerworld.com/managementtopics/outsourcing.

Evalueserve Business intelligence and market research firm with headquarters in New Delhi: www.evalueserve.com

Morgan Chambers Independent consultancy company Morgan Chambers specializes in all aspects of IT outsourcing and business process outsourcing: www.morgan-chambers.com.

National Outsourcing Association Europe's first association for effective business and process outsourcing, the National Oursourcing Association has recently launched the journal *Outsourcing*: www.noa.co.uk.

neoIT Consultancy firm neoIT provides a useful offshore knowledge centre: www.neoit.com/gen/knowledgecenter/knowledgecenter.html.

Offshore Development A directory to offshore companies worldwide: www.offshore-development.co.uk.

OffshoreITOutsourcing A resource for prospective buyers and sellers, providing access to a global network of pre-qualified vendors plus general information and advice: offshoreitoutsourcing.com.

OutsourcingCentral Provides access to an outsourcing information portal and the monthly *Outsourcing Provider Magazine*: www.outsourcingcentral.com.

OutsourcingCenter An outsourcing portal provided by the publishing and research division of consulting firm Everest Group. The site offers two monthly online publications, the *Outsourcing Journal* and *BPO Outsourcing Journal*: www.outsourcing-center.com.

Outsourcing Institute This US-based organization describes itself as the first and only global professional association dedicated solely to outsourcing: www.outsourcing.com.

Shared Services and Business Process Outsourcing Association A leading, independent, global body whose members include service providers and practitioners around the world: www.akris.com.

Sourcing Interests Group This group helps members to learn from each other's experiences in outsourcing, alliances, procurement, ecommerce and shared services: www.sourcinginterests.org.

Preface

Controversy surrounds the rapidly growing offshoring market. The use of global IT services offers the potential for compelling cost savings, but also brings increased risk of problems in communications, quality management and control. Media reports have highlighted some of the difficulties and the possible negative impact on UK jobs. However, companies operate in an increasingly competitive world and cannot afford to ignore a sourcing strategy that might deliver major benefits.

In this environment, few organizations are confident enough to talk openly about their offshore work. Maryfran Johnson, editor in chief of *Computerworld*, has written about the growing self-censorship around offshore sourcing and the stifling effect it is having on honest information exchange. 'At a time when more companies are gaining experience – both good and bad – with offshore firms and outsourcing contracts, fewer companies are going to be willing to share those experiences' (www.computerworld.com). In the UK, there are many conferences and seminars about offshore outsourcing, but these are invariably dominated by consultants and representatives from the offshore industry who understandably stress the advantages and benefits of offshoring.

I have written this book to give you an impartial and balanced analysis of the offshoring trend – advantages and benefits, risks and countermeasures – and guidelines for managing offshore projects. Although India is the major player in this global market, the offshore industry is growing in many other countries. Most books on offshoring concentrate on India, but I felt that it was important to look at a wide range of locations, each of which has its own strengths and weaknesses. In all, I describe 18 countries and give sources of further information for each destination.

Is offshoring right for your organization? How should you tackle an offshore project? Although there is no simple answer to these questions, my book aims to give you valuable advice, leading you to the information you need to make an objective assessment of global sourcing and manage offshore projects successfully.

Elizabeth Sparrow

1 Introduction

Welcome to the world of global sourcing. Standardized business applications, inexpensive bandwidth and web-based collaborative tools have opened up opportunities for less wealthy countries around the world to develop IT service industries and compete in the global market. Just as computer hardware manufacturing moved overseas in the 1970s and 1980s, the IT services industry is now migrating to countries such as India, China, the Philippines and South Africa. A wide range of business models is emerging as companies seek to exploit the benefits of offshore sourcing. UK companies may set up their own offshore IT centres or may choose to outsource to suppliers based overseas, or to European or American outsourcers who themselves have offshore subsidiaries.

Gartner has described the move towards offshore sourcing as an 'irreversible mega trend' (www.gartner.com). Companies are increasingly moving work overseas to cut costs and free up resources to focus on new business opportunities and innovation. Companies who fail to take advantage of the emerging global IT services industry may well lose out to those who do. Among European countries, the UK leads the way in adopting offshore sourcing. While this means that the UK's own IT sector will be the first to feel the impact on jobs, the country also has the opportunity to take the lead as it learns to adapt and benefit from the new global IT services market.

Although the range of technical skills available through offshore service providers is increasing, IT professionals in the UK will still be needed to work on new technologies, IT architecture, business process analysis, strategic planning and programme management. A set of new roles concerned with the management of outsourcing contracts will need to be developed further: relationship management, contract administration, service level monitoring and problem resolution.

The use of offshore services offers the potential for significant cost savings, but also brings increased risk of problems in communications, quality management and control. This management guide examines the advantages and disadvantages of offshore sourcing and provides advice on managing offshore contracts. It also looks at the offshore industry that has developed around the world, identifying the particular strengths within each country. Although written from a UK standpoint, this guide is intended to help everyone working in the world of global sourcing. For a quick introduction to offshore outsourcing and answers to some common misconceptions, see Offshore Outsourcing Question Time.

OFFSHORE OUTSOURCING QUESTION TIME

Doesn't low price mean low quality?

Not necessarily. The price paid for offshore IT services depends, among other things, on local wage rates, local infrastructure costs, local business taxes and currency exchange rates. Offshore IT professionals are relatively well paid in their own countries and some of the brightest and best-educated graduates are attracted to this work. Led by India, the offshore industry has emphasized the importance of sound quality management processes and many offshore suppliers have achieved compliance with internationally recognized quality standards.

How many IT jobs in the UK have been lost through offshoring?

We don't have precise figures for this and we probably never will. It's not possible to distinguish accurately between job reductions driven by increased efficiency or lower investment in IT and those lost because some work has been moved offshore. Some would argue that using offshore resources helps companies improve their competitiveness and in the long run this will lead to an increase in jobs.

Isn't it all just hype? At every outsourcing conference these days there seem to be offshore companies promoting their services. We never hear from customers about real world experiences, good and bad.

Undoubtedly overseas suppliers do sometimes over-emphasize their achievements. But newspapers tend to exaggerate problems with alarmist headlines. Unfortunately this discourages many companies from talking about their experiences, good and bad, and few are prepared to give presentations about their offshore projects. This is not helping us develop best practice and learn lessons from others' experiences.

My company prefers to keep all IT functions in-house, so why should we consider offshore outsourcing?

The trend towards using offshore resources is often misleadingly referred to as offshore outsourcing. In fact moving work offshore does not necessarily mean that it is outsourced (in other words transferred to an external service provider). Tesco is a good example. The supermarket has a policy of keeping IT functions in-house, but this has not stopped Tesco setting up its own IT support centre in India. I chose the title of this book carefully to reflect the fact that using offshore resources doesn't always mean outsourcing.

Aren't near-shore and offshore outsourcing two different things?

You will find different people using these terms in different ways. I define near-shore as a type of offshore outsourcing (see the Glossary).

'Near-shore' means different things to different people. I would probably describe Hungary as nearshore but not Russia. Would you? Multinational companies often have difficulty defining for themselves what is offshore and what is not. But they too are part of the trend that is seeing IT service work move away from richer economies towards developing countries.

Can offshore programmers do object-oriented programming?

In the 1990s offshoring was commonly used for low-level coding and system maintenance, not because overseas IT professionals were incapable of more complex work but because this represented the lowest risk in a new and largely untried method of sourcing IT services. The larger offshore service providers, especially those in India, now supply a wide range of services and skills. Although some offshore services are provided by developing countries who may not be able to afford to provide further education for all their citizens, IT professionals often receive training that matches the best in the world.

I know someone who started a company that offered offshore services but it folded because there just wasn't the business there. How can offshore outsourcing have a significant impact when there is very little work that is suitable for transferring overseas?

The current offshore industry is very fragmented. There are a few large suppliers and many small companies. We are now seeing a period of consolidation with mergers and acquisitions commonplace and some company failures. Overall, however, the offshore market is growing strongly. While it is true that some IT service work will probably remain in the UK, it would equally be wrong to dismiss offshore outsourcing as a passing fad.

Surely outsourcing has had its day and work is now being moved back in-house? And total IT outsourcing deals have largely been discredited.

Yes, some companies have moved work back in-house. But the figures for outsourcing speak for themselves. Gartner has reported that the outsourcing segment is outperforming the western European IT services market overall, growing by 3.1 per cent in 2004 and expected to increase 8 per cent annually by 2007. Speaking at the Spring 2004 symposium in Barcelona, Roger Cox, Gartner's managing vice president said, 'Last year saw a phenomenon in Europe. Out of 15 one billion US dollar mega-deals signed in 2003, 10 were awarded by Europe-based enterprises. Until 2003, Europe-based organizations had only signed a total of 14 mega-deals since 1989.' In Western Europe, the UK is the largest and most mature market, representing 35 per cent of the total European out-sourcing market in 2004. Germany/Switzerland/Austria account for 22.8

> per cent and France 12.8 per cent. Italy and the Nordic regions represent 7.7 per cent and 7.2 per cent respectively, while Spain and Portugal have 4.6 per cent of the total market (www.gartner.com).
>
> ### Isn't offshore outsourcing bad for the UK economy?
>
> It depends on your point of view. McKinsey and others have argued that using cheaper offshore resources boosts the national economy by helping companies to become more competitive and win more business. Global trade brings significant benefits to the UK. Exports of goods and services to India alone are already worth around £2.5 billion a year. Protectionist measures harm national economies by isolating industries and not encouraging them to become more efficient. Brazil's IT sector is still suffering from trade restrictions imposed until the mid-1990s that left the industry ill-prepared to compete with service providers in other parts of the world.
>
> On the other hand, some argue that cost reductions achieved by companies through offshoring do not benefit the wider economy. They point to a potential loss of skills in the UK workforce and higher unemployment leading to a reduction in income tax paid to the Treasury. The savings made through offshoring are always at risk from exchange rate fluctuations, and political instability in some countries poses additional security risks.
>
> Personally I support the former view and have written this book to help us get the best from the trend towards buying offshore IT services.

THE ORIGINS AND GROWTH OF THE OFFSHORE MARKET

To survive and prosper, commercial organizations are constantly seeking out ways to improve their competitiveness and efficiency. Industry commonly looks to cut costs by moving routine jobs to lower cost countries during periods of economic recession. Early offshore sourcing projects in the IT services industry began in the USA in the early 1990s when legacy system maintenance costs were reduced by setting up operations in Canada, Ireland and India.

Software development costs have risen significantly within organizations as systems have been introduced into every facet of business life and growing internet use has driven a new set of IT requirements. New software engineering techniques have evolved to cope with this mass of application development work – structured analysis and design, computer-aided tools, object-oriented programming and software components. While the volume of software development work continues to rise, these new techniques have opened up the possibility of parcelling up segments of application development work to be carried out offsite, possibly in another country.

Technological developments have made offshore working an increasingly viable option. Millions of miles of fibre cable have been laid around the world and the cost of global broadband connections has dramatically reduced. Both data and conventional telephony networks have increased rapidly in both quantity (bandwidth) and reliability. Internet-based email, newer collaborative working technologies and conventional telephony have combined to make it almost as easy to work with partners on the opposite side of the world as on a different floor of the same building.

The huge volume of work involved in modifying systems to ensure Year 2000 compliance boosted the offshore industry. There were severe skills shortages in the USA and Europe, particularly in technologies supporting older legacy systems (Cobol was a key example), and organizations found that Indian software companies were able to provide the necessary skills and were keen to undertake this sometimes tedious work at very competitive prices. Results were mixed and some organizations experienced telecommunications problems and had difficulties with immature processes and methodologies. Cultural differences between organizations in different countries also damaged understanding and coordination. Learning from these experiences, the major offshore players have improved service quality, developed processes to streamline offshore working and taken steps to mitigate risks.

Established outsourcing service providers are under pressure to reduce costs as profit levels have fallen across the industry. Software and services companies are setting up operations around the world, reducing costs where they can and spreading the risks of problems inherent in any one location by opening offices in many different countries. IDC has identified offshore outsourcing as the dominant trend in the IT services industry in the USA, Europe and Japan with over 40 per cent of application management contracts now having some offshore component. In the UK, IDC estimates that 60 to 80 per cent of the contract negotiations between large companies and suppliers now involve some element of offshore working.

In Europe, the enlargement of the European Union (EU) in 2004 to include countries such as the Czech Republic, Hungary and Poland has opened up new possibilities for the emerging offshore industry in Eastern Europe. The common EU approach to business and employment issues such as data protection reduces some of the risks associated with offshore outsourcing.

We are witnessing a shift from national to global IT services companies. Offshore suppliers are themselves outsourcing to cheaper locations and developing into major global organizations. Ovum Holway predicts that by 2010 one of today's leading offshore companies will make it into the global IT Top Ten.

The globalization of the IT services industry opens up new opportunities for IT professionals around the world. Increasingly we will find that major IT programmes will be carried out by project teams based in different countries and users will place more emphasis on performance and service levels than on the location of IT support staff. There has been much speculation about the impact of this globalization on job numbers. Ovum Holway has predicted that between 20,000 and 25,000 jobs may be lost in the UK IT industry over the next few years as a direct result of work moving offshore. Gartner has forecast that up to 25 per cent of traditional IT jobs will move offshore by 2010. While there is no doubt that new IT jobs will be created in emerging markets around the world, the impact on IT jobs in America and Europe is hard to predict accurately. Offshore sourcing can help organizations improve their competitiveness and free up resources for research and development. If the global economic recovery continues and strengthens, new demands, together with the introduction of new technologies, will lead to the creation of new IT jobs.

BUSINESS MODELS

As the global IT services industry develops, a rich mix of business models is evolving. There are many different ways to introduce offshore working into an overall sourcing strategy and, as illustrated in Table 1.1, this does not necessarily involve outsourcing. Some organizations prefer to set up their own IT centres in offshore locations (commonly referred to as 'captive' facilities) or to set up joint ventures with offshore companies.

Table 1.1 *Global delivery models*

Service responsibility	Delivery model
Retained in-house	Global IT departments
	Acquisitions
	Global organic growth
Shared	Shared services
	Joint ventures
	Alliances
Transferred to external service provider	Established multinational outsourcing companies
	Established offshore service providers
	Outsourcing companies specializing in offshore working
	Emerging offshore companies

Established multinational outsourcing companies

Some firms, such as IBM Global Services, CSC and EDS, are already well established in America and Europe and offer a wide range of IT services, supported by large teams with an extensive skills base. These suppliers are incorporating offshore resources into their commercial services. They have the scale to operate in several different countries to mitigate the risk of political or social instability at any one location. These companies have tried and tested outsourcing processes in place and have extensive experience in the market. This offers a relatively low-risk entry into offshore sourcing, but is not the cheapest option.

EDS BEST SHORE

Texas-based EDS is a leading global services company with annual earnings in excess of £11 billion. The company established its first offshore facility in 1990. The Best Shore initiative was launched in 2002 and integrates EDS's worldwide network of delivery capabilities to provide seamless onshore/near-shore/offshore application development and management services at competitive prices. EDS places work on the 'best shore' where it has developed capabilities which match the technology/industry expertise required by the client. This reduces the risk associated with specific locations. Best Shore builds on EDS's economies of scale, global infrastructure and the technical skills of more than 135,000 employees. With a worldwide network of 300 delivery facilities, EDS can offer full 24/7 'follow the sun' capabilities. 'EDS Best Shore offers our global clients exactly what they have asked for – consistently superior service around the world at competitive prices,' said Paulett Eberhart, president of EDS's Solutions Consulting line of business, when launching the service. 'Whether clients need applications development or delivery, or IT outsourcing or business process outsourcing, EDS can provide a consistent, seamless environment regardless of global location.'

By 2005, EDS expects to have over 20 facilities in 17 countries devoted to the Best Shore programme. Over 20,000 people will be working on the services. Current Best Shore facilities are based in Argentina, Australia, Brazil, Canada, the Czech Republic, Egypt, India, Ireland, Malaysia, Mexico, New Zealand and South Africa.

EDS itself has exploited the potential of global sourcing. The Chennai Solution Centre in India has teamed with US-based resources to support applications and databases for the majority of the company's internal human resources, billing, administrative and treasury systems. Following a rapid, eight-month implementation, EDS has achieved ongoing annual cost savings of about 36 per cent.

www.eds.com, www.computerworld.com, presentation by JACK NOBLE, EDS global solution architect to the BCS London (Central) Branch, October 2003

Established offshore service providers

Experienced offshore companies such as Tata Consultancy Services (TCS), Wipro and Infosys in India have well-developed outsourcing processes and can offer quality services at competitive prices. The major companies in this category employ international sales and support teams, which helps to overcome some of the problems caused by cultural differences between countries. The executives in these companies, however, do not necessarily have a good understanding of their client's business sector and commercial environment. More effort may be needed by both client and service provider to develop a mutual understanding of service requirements and an effective ongoing outsourcing relationship.

The leading offshore suppliers are expanding fast, widening the scope of services offered, opening offices in other countries and growing to become multinational service providers on a scale to match the major American and European companies.

> **THAMES WATER**
>
> *Computer Weekly* reported that the UK's largest water company (and number three in the world), Thames Water, cut its IT maintenance bill by more than £1 million or 20 per cent by outsourcing to Wipro in 2002. Wipro was adopted as lead partner in acceptance testing and is responsible for managing Thames Water's support and maintenance suppliers. When it comes to development projects, Wipro works alongside other suppliers.
>
> The deal with Wipro has also produced improvements in quality and innovation. 'I always try to put price last. It would be very easy to throw everything at India because it is cheap. And it is not because it is cheap – it is cost effective,' said Alasdair Macarthur, IS partner development manager at Thames Water. 'Savings of 20 per cent are a good start. But let's make it 25 per cent or 30 per cent. Let's use the full gamut of Wipro's quality accreditation to drive up quality.'
>
> In 2003 Thames Water signed a business process outsourcing deal with Xansa, which will see more than 700,000 metered billing exceptions and customer correspondence handled by Xansa's offices in India on behalf of Thames Water every year. The Swindon-based customer service systems will be accessed remotely from India. The service level agreement specifies that Xansa has to process correspondence within four days, 90 per cent of metered billing exceptions by day one and 100 per cent by day three.
>
> www.computerweekly.com

Outsourcing companies specializing in offshore working

Companies such as Cognizant and EPAM have their headquarters and top management team in America or Europe, but the majority of their staff are recruited and based overseas. This means that clients liaise within their own country with a company that has a good understanding of local issues and the business environment. These service providers are able to offer cheaper services than the established multinational companies but not the depth and range of services.

> **COLGATE**
>
> Colgate-Palmolive, a £5 billion company, markets products around the world under brands such as Colgate, Palmolive, Ajax, Fab and Mennen. To help sales representatives manage a large portfolio of customers, products and promotional material, Colgate wanted an application that provided on-demand, real-time information to every sales person in distributed office environments in 30 countries. They needed a sales-support system capable of disseminating data to multiple users and running a variety of databases on multiple hardware platforms.
>
> EPAM Systems, a company with its headquarters in Princeton, New Jersey and Budapest, Hungary and development centres in Russia and Belarus, developed a proprietary mobile application, known as LISA2, for Colgate-Palmolive. LISA2 not only provides the real-time information required, but also reduces costs by replacing the global paper mailing of tens of thousands of product updates and reports each month. With a laptop computer, a sales person can liaise with internal contacts, manage customer calls, manage and track sales targets, enter and monitor orders and process orders online. More than £2 billion in sales pass through the system each year, making LISA2 one of the most critical business systems at Colgate. 'Having a flexible system in place globally has allowed us to be more responsive to new business demands,' said Stefan Ziehrer, head of the Colgate Sales Support Competence Centre, Germany. 'We can confidently say that we are running our sales organization as productively as possible.'
>
> www.epam.com

Emerging offshore companies

As knowledge of the developing global IT services market spreads around the world, new companies are forming in many different countries. These organizations offer the cheapest prices, being keen to win business deals, but they have little experience. It may be difficult to establish their financial viability, exactly what they are capable of delivering and how reliable their services will be. This is clearly a higher-risk option and generally should be used only for small-scale, non-critical work.

Global IT departments

Large multinational companies have had local offices in different countries for many years. The same technological advances that have led to the growth in offshore outsourcing are also leading to a redistribution of application development and support work to those local IT departments able to recruit and retain qualified IT professionals most economically. Whereas in the past systems used in the UK would usually be developed in the UK, some of this work can now be done in another country.

> **SHELL**
>
> **Multinational oil firm Shell has launched a major initiative known as 'IT Vision' in which the company aims to achieve world-class price performance by 2008. Shell plans to rationalize its application portfolios and global infrastructure, streamline its decision-making and improve procurement processes. The global IT workforce, which currently stands at 9,300, will be reduced by 20 to 30 per cent. Shell plans to move work away from higher cost areas such as the UK, the Netherlands and the USA and take advantage of the cost savings to be gained from locating work in India and Malaysia. The company will expand its own IT centre in Cyberjaya, Malaysia and will also outsource some work to IBM and major Indian service providers including Wipro.**
>
> www.computing.co.uk, ANDREW HIGGINS,
> Communications Manager IT, Shell

Shared services

Within each industry sector there are certain business functions that are common to every organization and do not offer possibilities for competitive advantage. Some organizations, while continuing to compete for business, recognize the advantage of collaborating to reduce the cost of common business functions. By aggregating the requirement, economies of scale can be achieved. Shared service centres are set up to provide these common functions and these organizations may outsource business processes and IT support to offshore workers.

Joint ventures

Rather than transfer IT services to an offshore supplier, some companies prefer to set up a separate joint venture organization with an external service provider to gain access to offshore resources without losing control over the new IT operation. A commercial agreement specifies the objectives and targets for the new organization.

> **NEUSOFT AND PHILIPS**
>
> In June 2004 Neusoft Group of China and Royal Philips Electronics of the Netherlands officially launched a manufacturing and research and development joint venture for medical systems. The joint venture is known as Philips and Neusoft Medical Systems and will focus on developing and manufacturing medical imaging systems for the Chinese and international markets. Its headquarters are in Shenyang, north-east

> China and the company will be developing and manufacturing computed tomography and x-ray equipment, ultrasound and magnetic resonance imaging equipment, as well as picture archiving and communications systems products that are used to store radiology images. 'By joining forces with Neusoft', said Martin Schuurmans, executive vice president of Philips Medical Systems, 'Philips will leapfrog into the high-growth medical equipment market in China and sharpen the competitive edge by tapping into local know-how of application for that market.'
>
> www.neusoft.com

The joint venture has its own management team and draws on the resources of both parties, who share the costs and risks. One of the potential dangers inherent in this business model is that there may be no redress if targets are not met.

Alliances

An alternative approach is to set up a strategic alliance with an offshore service provider. A commercial agreement is formally drawn up, covering a range of activities in which the onshore and offshore organizations will cooperate. This may include shared software development, joint research teams, cross-marketing campaigns and integrated projects. Both organizations continue to operate as separate legal entities, however, and there is no separate, independent management team as set up within a joint venture.

> **NATIONAL HEALTH SERVICE**
>
> In a landmark achievement for India's TCS, the NHS appointed the Fujitsu alliance, of which TCS is a member, as a local service provider. The £896 million contract spread over nine years will help the NHS in its drive to improve healthcare for patients in southern England. TCS will provide clinical application implementation and data migration. Commenting on the win, Mr Ramadorai, chief executive officer of TCS said, 'We are delighted that our alliance has bagged the prestigious project from the National Health Service. We look forward to working closely with our alliance partners and providing our expertise in data management and application implementation to meet the goals of the project.'
>
> www.tata.com

Acquisitions

Some organizations, particularly the large American and European service providers, gain access to offshore resources by acquiring overseas companies. This is a quick way to incorporate the expertise and capabilities of offshore firms, but may require a lot of effort to integrate the cultures of two different companies and to develop and implement common processes that deliver quality IT services.

Global organic growth

Some of the major American and European IT service companies have expanded overseas through organic growth, setting up proprietary offshore facilities. This process takes longer than acquiring local overseas outsourcing firms, but can produce higher quality, more reliable service standards.

> **GLOBAL INSERVE FROM I-VANTAGE**
>
> i-Vantage provides end-to-end offshore solutions for IT, call centres and back office functions. The company's corporate headquarters are in Cambridge, Massachusetts and it has offices in Chicago, London, Ontario, Hyderabad and Kolkata (formerly Calcutta). i-Vantage's core services help organizations build their own offshore facilities in the form of joint ventures or fully owned subsidiaries.
>
> The Global InServe model provides a different approach to traditional offshore outsourcing. It offers the same processes that many major firms have used to create their own wholly owned subsidiaries offshore, staffed with their own employees and focused on driving down costs for outsourced operations so those companies can focus spending on growth and often new local jobs. i-Vantage helps its clients define the scope and requirements of their new offshore subsidiaries – called Global Delivery Centres – and create and file the necessary paperwork. i-Vantage also screens and interviews local candidates to its clients' job specifications. It modifies office space as required and provides an onsite coordinator. 'This is now possible in India because the talent pool is more mature, vertically literate, and finds working directly for clients much more attractive,' Ian Conway, director of business development and operations at i-Vantage told me. 'In fact, often the client wants to create a captive operation alongside its existing outsourcing contracts to maintain flexibility and create some competitive pressure.'
>
> www.i-vantage.com, IAN CONWAY

WORK PERMITS

Countries around the world adopt different policies towards the employment of foreign nationals. As part of the offshore sourcing process, clients may want to send some of their staff to the offshore destination to develop good personal working relationships and share business knowledge. Equally, the offshore company may wish to send some of its staff to their client's country to learn more about local culture and to develop expertise in their client's business systems. Arrangements for controlling the admission of foreigners to work in any country are therefore of interest and possible concern for the offshore services industry.

In the UK, any organization wanting to employ someone from beyond the European Economic Area (EEA) needs first to have advertised the job adequately in the UK. Any foreign national must be the best applicant for the job and receive the equivalent salary to a UK employee in the same post. There are exemptions to the advertising rule for skills that are in short supply. These are listed on the Home Office-approved skills shortage list. For these jobs work permits can be issued quickly and there is no obligation to advertise for UK recruits. In 2003, following submissions from the BCS demonstrating that there were no skills shortages (in fact a large number of UK professionals were unemployed) and pressure from the Professional Contractors' Group concerned about the number of contractors out of work, IT occupations were removed from the skills shortage list.

With intra-company transfers different rules apply. A foreign company with a UK subsidiary can bring in staff to work at that subsidiary without advertising. These employees must be paid at the same rate as their UK counterparts. The rules governing intra-company transfers do not apply to recruitment agencies.

These limitations do not apply to EU nationals who are free to work in any European country. EU expansion in 2004 may bring IT professionals from some of the new member states to Germany, France and the UK.

RESPONSES TO THE OFFSHORE OUTSOURCING TREND

The globalization of the IT services industry can be a deeply disruptive and challenging development for IT professionals. Companies that choose to send work overseas can seem callous and unappreciative of the contribution made by in-house staff. As economic, political and technological forces shape the global distribution of IT jobs some people feel that they have little control over their future IT careers. It is hardly surprising, then, that responses to offshoring are often emotional and governments are under pressure to curtail the increase in offshore outsourcing.

In the UK we expect, as citizens in a free, capitalist democracy, to be able to buy goods and services from the best source, whether that be a German car, a Japanese camera or a holiday cottage in France. We also value the opportunity to work in any EU country or perhaps to work in the USA for a time. Indeed IT professionals have enjoyed international careers for many years (the first president of the BCS, Sir Maurice Wilkes, joined the central engineering staff of the Digital Equipment Corporation in Maynard, Massachusetts in 1980 and worked in the USA until 1986). Companies also have the freedom to buy products and services from around the world so that they can remain competitive in the global market, protecting their stakeholders' interests.

One of the myths about offshore sourcing is that there is nothing more to the trend than a desire by some unscrupulous companies to pay low costs for services provided by workers earning low wages and producing shoddy work. This is far from accurate. Offshore IT professionals are relatively well paid compared to others in their own countries, highly educated and well motivated. IT jobs are prized and there is a strong commitment to developing the IT services industry.

The current increase in offshore sourcing has come at a difficult time, when IT jobs are not readily available in the UK and unemployment among IT professionals has risen. It is worth remembering, however, that just a few years ago demand for IT staff far outstripped supply. The need for IT professionals combining technical skills with business knowledge continues to increase and these jobs are less likely to move offshore. New areas such as bioinformatics and nanotechnology will grow in the future, drawing on the innovative skills of UK IT professionals.

A report from New Delhi-based research company Evalueserve has predicted that continued economic growth in the UK will create new jobs, but slow population growth and the effect of an aging population will lead to a shortfall in the labour supply. Evalueserve estimates that the gap between demand and supply in the UK will reach 714,000 jobs by 2010. Industries that will face the maximum shortfall are likely to be healthcare, IT and education. Global sourcing can help address this issue (see www.evalueserve.com).

A McKinsey Global Institute study challenged the perception that offshoring has a negative impact on the USA job market and the American economy. Technological change, economic recession and business restructuring often result in the loss of large numbers of jobs. The history of the US job market suggests that new jobs will be created to replace (and even exceed) those lost through outsourcing. The study also looked at the impact of the aging population. McKinsey estimated that America will need 5 per cent more workers by 2015 simply to maintain the current ratio of workers to the total population and the living standards enjoyed by today's citizens. Offshoring is one way to meet this need (see McKinsey Global Institute, 2003).

Trade union responses to offshore outsourcing

There are about 1 million IT professionals in the UK, but only 5 to10 per cent belong to a trade union. Most trade union members work in the finance and public services sectors. Unions representing IT professionals in the UK include:

- the white collar science and engineering union Amicus;
- the Communication Workers' Union (CWU);
- Unifi, whose members work in the financial services sector.

The unions have argued against the inevitability of sending work overseas and the need to offer retraining and support to those who lose their jobs through offshore outsourcing. They have been concerned about the impact on society at large (especially the large numbers of jobs lost at call centres).

Amicus

With over 1 million members drawn from both the private and public sectors, Amicus is the largest manufacturing union in the UK. In its offshoring campaign statement Amicus recognizes that technological progress has made change unavoidable:

> It is our job to best protect the interests of our members to make sure that we manage that change, within the context of a global economy, where nobody loses out. We are working with our sister trade unions in the UK and at the same time strengthening our contact with India trade unions.
>
> Amicus is leading a campaign that is looking to the future and looking to a modern world of work. When we use that phrase now we don't mean just the place in which we work but instead refer to our entire planet. Just as they say that the sun never sets on a paperless office, we need also to ensure that we deliver a modern progressive world of work where union members find solutions working in harmony with employers and government alike, right around the globe.

Visit www.amicustheunion.org for further information.

CWU

CWU is the largest union for the communications industry in the UK, with 300,000 members who work in the Post Office, BT and other telephone companies, cable TV, Accenture, the Alliance and Leicester and Girobank. Its pink elephant campaign opposes BT's plans to transfer work to India. According to the CWU research department:

> The seismic shift of labour from Europe and America has massive consequences for UK workers in the telecommunications and call centre industries. As many as 200,000 jobs could be at risk over the next 10 years.
>
> The CWU have made it clear that we have no argument with India or Indian workers. Our issue is with BT. BT is a UK company that derives its profits from UK customers and is therefore obliged to support the UK economy by employing UK workers.

Visit www.cwu.org for further information.

Unifi

Unifi has 158,000 members in over 400 organizations and is Europe's largest specialist finance sector trade union. It has been negotiating with employers in order to avoid compulsory redundancies resulting from offshore outsourcing. In January 2004, Unifi reached a benchmark agreement with Barclays, creating a framework to handle the bank's strategic options for outsourcing jobs abroad. The union accepted that Barclays needed to reorganize the business, while the bank recognized the union's need to protect the redeployment and job security of its members. Unifi represents over two-thirds of Barclays' 9,000 UK-based IT staff.

Ed Sweeney, Unifi's General Secretary said:

> All across the service sector we are seeing possible and actual job migration to areas where labour is significantly cheaper. Many companies are just jumping on the bandwagon; others have made rational strategic decisions. Trade unions must ensure that they can deal with any situation in order to protect their members' interests. A positive agreement such as the one we have entered into with Barclays is the only constructive way forward and will set a measure against which other companies looking to outsource from the finance sector will have to be tested.

The key elements of the agreement include the following:

- A voluntary redundancy register will be set up where jobs are being lost through offshore outsourcing or restructuring. Anyone working within a defined geographic area, whatever their business unit, can register their interest in voluntary redundancy.
- Job matching will enable those who have volunteered for redundancy to swap jobs at the same grade with those who have lost their jobs but do not want to be made redundant.
- Staff will be redeployed into vacant posts or roles filled by agency staff or contractors even if they do not possess all the skills required but there is a realistic chance of acquiring the skills through additional training. A one- to three-month trial period will be allowed for this training.
- Money will be made available for external career retraining where no redeployment option can be found.
- External, independent support will be provided for those who are developing new careers, whether inside Barclays or in other organizations.

Visit www.unifi.org.uk for further information.

Professional and trade association responses

British Computer Society

The British Computer Society (BCS) aims to be the UK's leading professional and learned society in the field of computers and information systems with members in over 100 countries around the world. It is working to make the IT profession the key profession of the 21st century by:

- setting the standards for IT;

- developing cutting-edge products and services;
- encouraging IT professionals to continuously develop their skills and competences;
- informing and influencing individuals, organizations and government on key issues;
- initiating debate on strategic IT issues;
- providing international support.

The BCS has issued a position statement on offshore outsourcing that recognizes the significant benefits that can be derived:

> UK companies will want to exploit the advantages offered by offshore outsourcing services to maintain their competitiveness in the global marketplace. The British Computer Society promotes the exploitation of IT to deliver maximum business benefit and recognizes that attempts to regulate the market will ultimately harm British interests.

As well as leading to job losses in the UK, the BCS envisages that the offshore trend will influence wages:

> We anticipate an impact on UK IT salary levels, which rocketed to unsustainable levels in the late 1990s. In the past even junior, inexperienced IT staff could command very high wage rates but we are unlikely to see a return to this situation. Salary levels in developing countries such as India may well rise as their IT service industries develop, but for many years to come there will be countries able to offer quality services at low costs.
>
> The British Computer Society will be monitoring the impact of the growth in offshore outsourcing and reviewing a number of areas including:
> - A renewed focus on quality management processes in UK-based IT organizations.
> - Identifying and developing the skills needed by UK IT staff so that they can add value that cannot be matched by offshore workers.
> - Promoting the competitive strengths of UK IT professionals, especially in leading edge, innovative technologies.
> - Encouraging organizations and government to retrain and redeploy any IT professionals who find themselves without work as a result of offshore outsourcing.

Chief executive David Clarke has said:

> I don't believe there is any way we can regulate the market by legislation. I believe that market forces will prevail in the UK, but we can and must compete. As with all successful marketing campaigns, we must find our unique selling points and make sure decisions are made on these criteria – not the competition's strengths.

Visit www.bcs.org for further information.

Professional Contractors' Group

The Professional Contractors' Group (PCG) was formed in 1999 to represent independent contractors and consultants in lobbying against the UK government's IR35 (tax) proposals. It has evolved into a professional body concerned with all issues affecting independent freelancers. Just over a half of its members are IT professionals.

The PCG has been much concerned about the work permit scheme that allows firms to bring non-EU workers into the UK, if they cannot recruit suitably qualified UK-based IT professionals. According to the PCG, abuse of intra-company transfers leaves a loophole in the system. It claims that many firms are now abusing the intra-company transfer system by bringing in large numbers of overseas workers and exploiting them by paying less than the going rate. PCG says that it has evidence that IT workers are coming into the UK without genuine company specific skills, in fact they are often trained in the UK after arriving, and are replacing UK IT professionals rather than filling vacancies:

> PCG believes that with so many experienced staff out of work, retraining of resident staff would in most cases be a viable alternative to bringing in overseas personnel. But while the work permits route provides a source of cheap labour, there will be little incentive for UK employers to provide the necessary investment in training. This will have serious long-term consequences for the IT industry, as it is de-skilled and foreign competitors' staff are trained in new technologies, which in turn assists the process of taking entire IT projects outside the UK.

Visit www.pcg.org.uk for further information.

National Outsourcing Association

The UK-based National Outsourcing Association (NOA) is Europe's first association for effective business and process outsourcing and parent of the European Outsourcing Association. Its members are companies who have outsourced (or are about to outsource) significant business processes or infrastructure, as well as the suppliers and legal/consultancy/service companies that support the industry. NOA operates as a trade association, an independent not-for-profit body whose objective is to leverage effective business and process outsourcing by promoting best practice and innovation; lobbying national governments, regulators and the EU; disseminating information and communicating the benefits of business outsourcing.

NOA believes that scare stories in the press have exaggerated the negative impact of offshore outsourcing:

> Whipping up a moral panic among the British public could be detrimental for business, confidence in the economy and public spirit. Offshoring is a fact – many companies are going to do it, whether there is public

> confidence behind the moves or not, but the effects of it will not be as dramatic as are being predicted.

A survey of NOA members suggests that growth in offshore outsourcing will be conservative, with the market growing steadily by 25 to 35 per cent a year. NOA sees global benefits flowing from the offshore industry.

> Business being shared on an international basis will have a positive effect on the growth of the global economy. IT will provide jobs in developing countries like India and China and give them the opportunity to compete on the world stage.

Visit www.noa.co.uk for further information.

Intellect

Intellect (formed from the merger of the Computing Services and Software Association and the Federation of the Electronics Industry) represents the UK's IT, telecommunications and electronics sectors. It aims to accelerate industry growth and prosperity, work with the government on behalf of the industry and raise media awareness of the significance of IT. The Intellect Offshore Group provides networking opportunities, education and market information to companies offering offshore software services to the UK market. It aims to promote offshore sourcing within the UK business community.

The trend towards offshore IT working is a relatively recent phenomenon and many companies have little experience on which they can draw. With the rapid market growth there are many companies touting for business, but the quality and reliability of services offered varies considerably. The Offshore Group has devised an Offshore Code of Practice to which all its members are committed. Clients can look to Intellect to help resolve any issues or concerns raised by the performance of any company that has signed up to the Code of Practice (see Appendix).

One of Intellect's current campaigns, 'Enabling the UK Knowledge Driven Economy', has identified the development of the global market as a key factor influencing the UK industry:

> To create a knowledge driven economy the UK must be able to compete within the developing global market place of the networked world. However, the UK's value proposition is not always competitive when measured against other countries – we are unable to compete on price with low cost production centres such as China, and we are losing our competitive advantage in high value add to countries such as India, USA and Australia.

Offshore outsourcing presents both threats and opportunities for UK-based companies, 'There is no preventing the trend – the only option is to raise the bar on the UK proposition.' In relation to the emerging markets in

India, China and elsewhere, 'Unless the infrastructure, skills and applications are in place to facilitate a competitive remote offering from the UK the threat exists that companies will redirect investment from the UK to these markets.'

Nick Kalisperas, director of the public sector team, told me:

> We are working to identify the value proposition offered by UK companies in the global market place. What we need now is joined up action from different government departments.

Visit www.intellectuk.org for further information.

Confederation of British Industry

The Confederation of British Industry (CBI) represents companies from all sectors of UK business. It is the leading organization representing UK firms, with its direct corporate members employing over four million and trade association membership representing over six million workers. The CBI has urged the government to adopt policies aimed at boosting skills, innovation and international trade. In his 2004 New Year message, Director-General Digby Jones said:

> We can no longer simply benchmark Britain against other major industrialized economies. We will increasingly find countries such as India and China competing for investment, not just because they offer cheaper labour but because they also have highly skilled people.

The impact of global competition will become more apparent as it spreads out beyond manufacturing: 'We can also expect more offshoring as firms rightly look for more effective ways of doing things.'

There are concerns about employment levels. Although the CBI predicts a growth in the job market in 2004, many of the new jobs will be in the public sector, while employment in manufacturing continues to fall.

The CBI has urged the government to develop an enterprise culture, building on Britain's macro-economic stability, use of the global business language, expertise as a trading nation and trust earned in global markets. Digby Jones said:

> Change and uncertainty are key challenges of globalization. We must rise to meet them with a bigger push towards more enterprise and greater competitiveness. Resisting the inevitable with more protectionism, more regulation and a siege mentality is a mug's game.

Visit www.cbi.org.uk for further information.

Government Responses

The Department of Trade and Industry (DTI) issued a consultation paper in 2003 in which it noted that quantifying the economic impact of offshore outsourcing on the UK or trying to predict the impact on jobs is very difficult. International trade in services has been increasing in recent years but, interestingly, the UK is a net beneficiary. The UK's service exports are £15 billion greater than its imports, and the UK is the world's second largest exporter of services. Overall, the paper argues, international competition creates jobs in the UK.

Secretary of State for Trade and Industry, Patricia Hewitt, wrote:

> We must focus all our effort on keeping the UK economy strong and stable, generating more jobs and better jobs by raising skill levels, supporting enterprise and raising innovation and productivity in business.
>
> As developing countries become richer, they will also buy more from us and invest more in our economy. UK exports of goods and services to India alone are already worth around £2.5 billion a year, securing thousands of UK jobs. But global trade – while making the UK as a whole richer – can have painful effects on the people and businesses who face new international competition. Our task as a government is to protect our people without lapsing into protectionism.
>
> The government believes that the global trade in services will bring significant benefits to the UK. However, it acknowledges that there may be short-term adjustment costs and will stand ready to help those affected.'
>
> www.dti.gov.uk

Speaking to author Mark Kobayashi-Hillary at the National Association of Software and Services Companies (NASSCOM) conference in 2004, minister for energy, ecommerce and postal services Stephen Timms said:

> We see the development of these partnerships with India as an important asset for UK firms and the UK economy. However, there are many concerns about outsourcing. There are people who feel there are threats on the horizon, so the DTI has been bringing people together from industry and the trade unions to investigate this. There is a consensus from our research that clearly indicates protectionism is not the right way forward for the UK.
>
> www.computing.co.uk.

Offshore outsourcing in Europe may be given a boost by the expansion in EU membership. Under the European Commission procurement rules, all public sector contracts must be offered in open competition to any EU company. Adverts are placed in the *Official Journal of the European Community* (*OJEC*) for all contracts with a value that exceeds a set threshold. Outsourcing suppliers in Eastern Europe are probably not yet sufficiently well organized to win a major German, French or British public authority contract. But this may change in future years as countries such as Hungary, the Czech Republic and Poland invest in and develop IT services industries.

> **LONDON CONGESTION CHARGING SCHEME**
>
> Capita Group is the UK's leading provider of integrated professional support service solutions. In less than 18 months, Capita designed and implemented the technology behind Transport for London's (TfL) Congestion Charging Scheme. The scheme was introduced to achieve one objective: to deter unnecessary car use within central London and thereby reduce congestion. The project involved over 450 man-years of development activity, leading to the introduction of the scheme in February 2003 on time and on budget. Capita now administers the image-gathering, sales channels and database interactions on behalf of TfL. Capita Group won the prestigious Social Contribution Award for its development of the London Congestion Charging Scheme at the BCS 2003 Information Technology awards.
>
> Mumbai-based Mastek was contracted by Capita to support the development of bespoke applications and the integration of key business applications, including an ecommerce website, call centre software and the image management system, as well as the integration of key external service providers.
>
> www.capita.co.uk, www.mastek.com, SUNIL MASRA, Mastek partnerships and alliances

The rapid growth in offshore outsourcing has sparked controversy and debate in 2004, the US presidential election year. At the time of writing (April 2004) it is not possible to predict with certainty how a future USA government will respond to the offshoring trend. Some congressmen, including presidential candidate Senator John Kerry (Democrat, Massachusetts), have proposed legislation to require companies to publicly disclose when they intend to move jobs offshore; or to restrict public sector contracts being undertaken offshore; or to prevent government assistance being given to companies favouring offshore workers over US employees. But even those at the centre of the arguments, like Senator Christopher Dodd (Democrat, Connecticut) have recognized that the trend towards offshore outsourcing cannot be stopped altogether, it may just be slowed down. Most of the proposed legislation concerns federal and state contracts and public sector work represents a very small proportion of the global IT services market.

At a joint news conference in Delhi with India's external affairs minister, Yashwant Sinha, Colin Powell, US Secretary of State said:

> Outsourcing invariably does result in the loss of jobs, and we have to do a better job in the United States, a good job in the United States, of creating opportunity in the United States to provide more jobs, so that those who have lost jobs will have opportunities in the future. It is the reality of 21st-century international economics that these kinds of dislocations will take place.
>
> www.computerworld.com

In some US states, plans to use offshore resources in government contracts have run into problems. The Indiana Department of Workforce Development cancelled a £8.4 million contract with TCS as part of an initiative to give companies and workers in Indiana a better chance to win state contracts. Public pressure forced New Jersey to bring back a helpline for welfare recipients that had been outsourced to India. Washington State Health Care Authority awarded a contract for developing an insurance benefits administration system to a company whose bid was £1.6 million cheaper than any other bid received and depended on using offshore workers. The winning bid was the only one received that fell within the budget limit set by the legislature. But the project did not progress to plan and ran over budget, prompting the proposed legislation to prevent government contracts being carried out by offshore workers.

Speaking at Boston College's Finance Conference 2004, Federal Reserve chairman Alan Greenspan argued that efforts to stem the tide of overseas outsourcing could damage the US economy instead of helping to protect American workers:

> We can erect walls to foreign trade and even discourage job-displacing innovation. The pace of competition would surely slow, and tensions might appear to ease – but only for a short while. Our standard of living would soon begin to stagnate and perhaps even decline as a consequence. Time and again through our history, we have discovered that attempting merely to preserve the comfortable features of the present – rather than reaching for new levels of prosperity – is a sure path to stagnation.
>
> news.zdnet.co.uk

Trade organizations are urging the government not to pass legislation that places restrictions on the use of offshore outsourcing. The Information Technology Association of America (ITAA) is concerned about difficulties this would cause US companies trying to sell IT services abroad. According to Harris Miller, president of the ITAA, 'It hurts our efforts to convince governments around the world to open their competition.' www.computerworld.com. A controversial report issued by the ITAA in 2004 claimed that although more IT jobs would be created offshore than in the USA in coming years, overall the US economy would benefit from the savings that outsourcing yields. The report suggested that 516,000 extra jobs would be created by the software and IT services sector between 2004 and 2009, of which 272,000 would go offshore. Although IT jobs had been lost as a result of offshoring, the productivity gains achieved lead to a net gain of 317,000 new jobs in other sectors by 2008. (www.itaa.org). Others have argued that the USA could be losing some of its best paying jobs and gaining lower paying ones.

The Computer Systems Policy Project, whose members include chief executives from Intel, Dell and Hewlett Packard, issued a report in 2004 emphasizing the need to maintain free international trade. Measures to constrain trade and collaboration often backfire. The report said:

> **Countries that resort to protectionism end up hampering innovation and crippling their industries, which leads to lower economic growth and, ultimately, higher unemployment.**
>
> www.news.com

2 Advantages and Benefits

Offshore sourcing can offer many benefits, most notably the opportunity to make substantial savings. Whereas, once, one programmer might have defined requirements, written code, tested the program and provided user support, today large projects are well defined and segmented into tasks that are carried out by different teams of professionals. We are quite accustomed to the teams working from different locations. Few IT departments – at least in medium-sized and large companies – have all their staff based at the same site as all users. To transfer some work to another country is, in some ways, not such a significant change.

In this chapter we look at the benefits of offshore outsourcing, listed in Table 2.1, based on today's economic conditions and technologies. As the global market in IT services develops the benefits will change. Salary levels will fluctuate and some countries will charge more for their services though competition will temper increases and there are plenty of countries lining up to compete for offshore business. Some functions might return as technology develops, for example, as speech recognition software improves, call centres and helpdesk services might benefit from greater automation and prove more economical to operate onshore. Nothing stands still – and the possible benefits from offshore sourcing are no exception. But the move towards a global market in IT services is a fundamental and far-reaching change. Companies will be able to scan the world for the best services at the best prices, not limited by national or international boundaries.

COST REDUCTION

The key driver behind the growth in offshore outsourcing is reduced costs. These derive primarily from the difference in wage levels in different

Table 2.1 *Advantages of offshore sourcing*

Cost reduction and other economic advantages
Quality management processes
'Follow the sun' operations
Access to skills and resources
In-house focus on core objectives
Productivity and service improvements
Support for business transformation and new development work

countries. It would be quite wrong, however, to compare this to low-cost manufacturing that depends on overseas sweatshops in which employees are poorly paid and work in unsatisfactory, even dangerous, factories. IT professionals working in the offshore industry are well paid and highly educated in comparison with other employees, enjoy working environments that compare favourably with those in the UK and have a relatively high standard of living in their own countries. There is often stiff competition for vacancies in offshore service providers.

We cannot extrapolate the savings achieved through offshore outsourcing simply from differences in salary levels. In many ways there has been too much focus on wage rates in the debate on offshoring. The savings a company can make by using offshore workers depends on:

- The country in which offshore work is carried out.
- The sourcing model adopted. For example, major IT companies with offshore subsidiaries generally charge higher prices than local offshore companies, but can offer other benefits.
- The proportion of onshore to offshore work – some work, especially tasks involving close interaction with users, needs to be carried out in the home country. More work sent offshore means greater savings, but other factors need to be taken into account – risk management, knowledge transfer and the need to maintain overall control.
- Management overheads – there are costs involved in managing any outsourcing contract. Cutting back on this function is a false economy that can lead to additional problems and expenditure. Effective management of offshore projects costs about 10 per cent of the overall contract value.
- Process improvements introduced as part of the offshoring programme.
- Productivity levels at the offshore company.

Estimates of overall savings achieved through offshoring vary considerably but are generally predicted to be in the range 25 to 40 per cent. Organizations interested in deriving the benefits of offshore working will find a discrete pilot or small-scale application development helpful in assessing the level of savings likely to be achieved without incurring high up-front costs.

EASYCINEMA

The Easy group of companies made substantial savings by using an offshore company to develop an online ticketing system successfully for easyCinema. *Computing* reported that Wipro, the Indian IT services company, was able to offer a saving of 45 per cent compared with the cheapest onshore bid for the contract. According to Easy group Chief Technology Officer, Phil Jones, 'Managing an offshore company is not as easy as managing an onshore company, but the savings were significant enough for us to want to do it. We also felt that it was strategically important to get experience of managing offshore companies.'

Tickets for easyCinema in Milton Keynes can be purchased on the web or using terminals at the cinema. Filmgoers receive bar-coded tickets that are scanned as they enter the cinema, so that the whole process is automated. Payment can be by card or cash, which is exchanged for tokens. Customers can also charge up accounts with online tokens so that children, for example, can get cinema tickets without further payment.

This system development project cost significantly less than other similar projects undertaken by the Easy group. The company will consider both onshore and offshore companies for future contracts.

www.computing.co.uk

OTHER ECONOMIC ADVANTAGES

With the focus on cost savings, other financial advantages that can be gained through offshoring may not be so immediately apparent. We have already seen that salary costs are much lower in many offshore destinations. Infrastructure costs, on the other hand, are largely constant around the world (for example, server prices and software license fees do not vary significantly between countries). In business cases supporting onshore IT projects we are used to seeing relatively high staff costs and low infrastructure costs. For offshore projects this balance is reversed. Projects that were once considered to be of little value can become financially attractive if the work is carried out overseas. Payback periods can be shorter and resource-intensive initiatives can become viable with the much lower salary costs incurred offshore.

Countries aiming to expand the local offshore services sector will often offer incentives to organizations relocating offices or setting up subsidiaries overseas. This might include a package of tax incentives and favourable employment regulations. Some countries have a reputation for overly bureaucratic government procedures, but special provision is often made to ensure that IT service providers setting up overseas operations suffer no unnecessary delays. These factors all need to be taken into account when assessing the cost of offshore working.

REUTERS

The global information, news and technology group Reuters has established software development centres in Bangalore and Bangkok. The centre in Thailand was formally opened in January 2002. Reuters invested £650,000 to set up a state-of-the-art facility capable of accommodating 200 software development, testing and project management professionals. Responsibility for some software applications has been transferred from Reuters' development locations in New York, Tokyo, Palo Alto and Sydney to Bangkok. The Thai centre works on real-time financial applications for market data display and analysis, order routing, transaction processing, news content creation and data distribution. Both experienced IT professionals and new graduates from university technology courses are recruited to work at the centre, which incorporates an in-house training facility and organizes regular software and process improvement courses.

'Reuters is investing in this facility because of our very positive experience with software development in Thailand. The skill and professionalism of our Thai development work is world-class,' said Todd Masters, technical director of Reuters Software (Thailand). 'We have received tremendous support from the Thai Board of Investment and look forward to returning that support by bringing employment, technology and training to Thailand.'

Reuters is consolidating its global software development operations as part of a £440 million cost-cutting programme and this will lead to job losses in London, Nottingham and elsewhere but an increase in staff numbers in Bangkok and Bangalore.

www.reuters.com, www.computing.co.uk

QUALITY MANAGEMENT

Offshore working has the potential to offer more than just cost advantages. IT professionals employed in the offshore industry tend to be educated to a higher academic level than their colleagues employed in similar jobs in the USA and Western Europe. Because wage levels are lower, offshore service providers are also able to invest in training and infrastructure and still undercut onshore outsourcing suppliers.

Early offshore projects were often bedevilled by poor quality and difficult communications. Realizing the importance of improving standards and establishing a reputation for good quality, the Indian offshore industry in particular has invested heavily in setting up excellent quality management processes and complying with international standards. The major Indian suppliers have typically reached a higher level of certification than companies in other countries. Common qualifications achieved by the leading offshore companies include ISO 9000, the Capability Maturity Model (CMM) and Six Sigma.

ISO 9000

The family of ISO 9000 standards, created and maintained by the International Standards Organization (ISO) helps companies of all types and sizes to implement and operate effective quality management systems:

- ISO 9000 describes the foundations of quality management systems and defines terminology.
- ISO 9000–3 looks at the application of the standards to software development and maintenance.
- ISO 9001 specifies the quality management systems needed by firms who have to demonstrate their ability to meet customer and regulatory requirements and improve customer satisfaction.

The standard identifies eight quality management principles that can be used to improve performance:

- a focus on customer needs, both current and future;
- a vision and environment, created by an organization's leaders, in which everyone can be fully involved in working towards the organization's objectives;
- recognition of the importance of the contribution that people at all levels make;
- the advantage of managing activities and resources as a process;
- the value of identifying, understanding and managing interrelated processes as a system;
- the importance of striving for continual improvement;
- the effectiveness of decisions based on an objective analysis of information;
- the added value derived from the development of mutually supportive relationships between an organization and its suppliers.

As the ISO 9000 standards have been adopted nationally in many countries (in the UK as BS 5750), there is growing worldwide interest in certification to demonstrate compliance. The ISO organizes the certification service and licenses accreditation bodies to authorize other professional organizations as certification bodies. These certification bodies perform the actual certification audits and confirm those organizations that qualify. These audits are repeated regularly to confirm continued compliance.

Capability Maturity Model

Pittsburgh-based Carnegie Mellon University's Software Engineering Institute (SEI) devised this model to describe an organization's ability to exert quality control and improve the productivity of its processes. The model is based on the following principles:

- Quality control and productivity can be improved by applying management methods based on quantitative analysis.
- The five-level capability model helps organizations to evaluate their achievements and identify areas for improvement.
- The processes defined at each level are generic and define the 'what' rather than the 'how' so that they can be applied to many different organizations.

The initial version of CMM was released in 1992. A number of variants were developed after 1993 for specific aspects of software development and maintenance:

- System Engineering CMM (SE-CMM) relates to product development and production of the developed product;
- Trusted CMM (T-CMM) focuses on sensitive and classified software systems;
- System Security Engineering CMM (SSE-CMM) covers security issues and secured product development processes;
- People CMM (P-CMM) relates to human resource development in software organizations;
- Software Acquisition CMM (SA-CMM) covers issues relevant to software purchased from external organizations such as contract monitoring and risk management.

When different variants of the CMM model were introduced in the same organization this caused difficulties in coordination and cooperation over joint processes. SEI therefore decided in the late 1990s to change direction in the development of CMM and began to integrate the variant models to produce the Capability Maturity Model Integration (CMMI) model illustrated in Table 2.2.

Among the 70 or so companies worldwide that have been publicly acknowledged as reaching the standard of CMM Level 5, about 50 are in India (www.computerworld.com). Compliance with these rigorous software development standards is a key marketing tool for these suppliers. Research carried out by SEI and Gartner has demonstrated that organizations with higher CMM ratings produce fewer software defects and complete projects on time more often.

Customers need to be aware, however, that CMMI Level 5 suppliers may expect their clients to work at the same level. Organizations used to working at, say, levels 1 or 2 will have few formal processes in place and may be unaccustomed to collecting and analysing quantitative data. Yet to work effectively with a Level 5 supplier this is what they may have to do. Some major Indian companies adapt their approach to suit their clients but this, of course, loses some of the benefits of working with a Level 5 supplier. As we have seen, the CMM standards specify what must be done

Table 2.2 *CMMI levels (derived from Galin, 2004)*

Capability maturity level	Process areas (PAs)
1. Initial	None
2. Managed	Requirements management
	Project planning
	Project monitoring and control
	Supplier agreement management
	Measurement and analysis
	Process and product quality assurance
	Configuration management
3. Defined	Requirements development
	Technical solution
	Product integration
	Verification
	Validation
	Organizational process focus
	Organizational process definition
	Organizational training
	Integrated project management
	Integrated teaming
	Risk management
	Decision analysis and resolution
	Organizational environment for integration
4. Quantitatively managed	Organizational process performance
	Quantitative project management
5. Optimising	Organizational innovation and deployment
	Causal analysis and resolution

rather than how it should be done. So customers should always consider carefully whether or not the processes suggested by their supplier best suit their business needs.

Any organization seeking accreditation to CMM standards must be independently assessed. The SEI advises that a published assessment is valid for two years, after which the accreditation needs to be repeated.

Visit www.sei.cmu.edu for further information.

INFOSYS TECHNOLOGIES

Bangalore-based Infosys Technologies completed an appraisal across development centres in India and several client locations in the USA in October 2003 and was assessed at CMMI Level 5. 'Infosys is continuously seeking to improve and maintain world-class quality in its operations across its own centres as well as at client locations,' said Satyendra Kumar, Head-Quality at Infosys Technologies. 'Our passion for quality has led to the successful completion of yet another CMMI appraisal where we have been rated again at Level 5. It is an honour and encourages us to strive harder for constantly excelling in quality standards and processes, which we believe are critical components for competitive success.'

Infosys has pioneered the implementation of the CMMI model at offsite and onsite centres. The 2003 appraisal was conducted by US-based Software Technology Transition from Bangalore, New Jersey and Chicago, covering projects from 14 client locations in the USA and 7 Infosys development centres.

www.infosys.com

COGNIZANT

KPMG carried out an independent assessment of Cognizant development centres in India, the USA and Europe and the Level 5 accreditation was announced in November 2003. By introducing CMMI processes, Cognizant reduced variations in achievement against design plan by 14 per cent, resulting in a 16 per cent improvement in the overall time-to-market for their clients. Undetected design defects were reduced by 7 per cent and this resulted in a 27 per cent improvement in the overall quality of deliverables. Substantial productivity and quality improvements have also been achieved over the years as Cognizant implemented CMM quality standards.

Cognizant's assessment covered 12 development centres – 10 in India based in Chennai, Bangalore, Kolkata (formerly Calcutta), Pune and Hyderabad and one each in Limerick and Phoenix, Arizona. It is among the largest assessments carried out.

Lead KPMG assessor, Veeraraghavan Kannan said, 'Cognizant has consistently demonstrated enterprise-wide process maturity, beginning with the company's first certification against the ISO framework in 1996. In each of our assessments Cognizant has illustrated a consistent focus on how CMM adds value to Cognizant's clients through quantitative systems performance enhancements and continuous process improvements.'

www.cognizant.com

Six Sigma

Advocates of Six Sigma claim very impressive financial benefits through adopting this continuous development programme. The name Six Sigma is based on the Greek letter sigma, which is used in statistical data to mean standard deviation. If you improve the sigma or standard deviation of any process you are in effect reducing the rate of defects or failure to meet specifications. Six Sigma aims to deliver a quality level of 3.4 defects per million opportunities (DPMO). This is close to an accuracy level of 99.999 per cent.

The basic aim of Six Sigma is to improve average performance and to reduce the variability of performance. A combination of established analytical techniques is used to set continuous improvement targets and monitor progress in improving any process. Six Sigma consists of a set of data-driven tools and methodologies. It is highly customer driven in that you cannot use the tools without taking customer needs into account. Multidisciplined project teams working on quality improvement in Six Sigma follow the DMAIC process – Define, Measure and Analyse, Improve and Control. The process consists of a series of standard activities and expected outputs.

As well as setting a high quality target, Six Sigma can be seen as a mechanism for building a culture of excellence as well as delivering financial benefits. Organizations implementing Six Sigma often train a large number of their employees in these techniques – there are even recognized levels of expertise: Black Belts (fully trained, full-time advisors), Green Belts (less training, part-time on Six Sigma projects) and Master Black belts who are site experts and trainers.

WIPRO

Wipro has one of the most mature Six Sigma programmes in the industry and was the pioneer of the methodology in India. The company has built up a skills base of over 120 black belts and over 3,350 employees have been trained in Six Sigma techniques. Wipro uses the DSSS (Development of Six Sigma Software) methodology for software development, which uses rigorous in-process metrics and cause analysis throughout the software development life cycle for defect-free deliveries and lower application development costs for customers. The company reports that this has enabled it to reduce software defects by 50 per cent and to cut life cycle times by reducing the need for re-working from 12 per cent to 5 per cent. Productivity is up by 35 per cent and installation failures in the hardware business are down from 4.5 per cent to 1 per cent. The lower application development costs have produced tangible cost savings for the customer.

www.wipro.com

FOLLOW THE SUN

Offshore centres are based in many different countries around the world in different time zones. This can be exploited to extend the working day, even as far as 24-hour working, without any office remaining at work during the night. Two examples illustrate the possibilities:

Example 1: Application development

Business analysts working on a project in Bristol have specified some last-minute adjustments that need to be made to a new system to be demonstrated to the company's marketing director the following day. In the late afternoon they call the project manager at home in Bangalore and send an email confirming the details.

When the application development team in Chennai arrive for work the following morning (when the business analysts are still asleep in Bristol) they are instructed by the project manager to make the necessary changes and configure the amended system ready for the demonstration in London.

In the afternoon in India, the business analysts arrive at work in Bristol. They work through the updated system and run through their presentation to make sure that everything works OK. They still have concerns about some of the on-screen information but they have time to brief their colleagues in London who are getting ready for the marketing director's arrival in the afternoon.

Example 2: Helpdesk

A virtual team whose members are based in Budapest, Mexico City and Hong Kong provides a helpdesk service. Each helpdesk office works an eight-hour shift as illustrated in Table 2.3.

All members of the helpdesk team use the same management system to get access to current availability information and to record calls received, problems resolved and advice given. The system is operated from a data

Table 2.3 *The virtual helpdesk*

GMT	Office at work, local time
7 am—3pm	Budapest, 8 am—4 pm
3 pm—11pm	Mexico City, 9 am—5 pm
11 pm—7am	Hong kong, 7 am—3 pm

centre in Nottingham. The users are based in offices in Birmingham, New York, Perth and Auckland. Whatever the time of day or night they can contact the helpdesk and whoever deals with their query will know if there are any problems with the service and will be aware of any previous calls they have made. This service is provided without any member of the helpdesk team having to work through the night.

ACCESS TO SKILLS AND RESOURCES

The emerging global offshore market is taking advantage of the large numbers of well-educated young people in India, China and elsewhere. Eastern European countries have highly skilled IT professionals that once would have worked for the state but now find it hard to get employment. In contrast, wealthier countries such as the UK have aging populations and will increasingly find it necessary either to allow more immigration or to move work offshore.

An important factor in outsourcing (and this is not limited to offshore companies) is that IT outsourcing suppliers specialize in IT – it is their core business. They carry out extensive training and invest in developing sound processes and methodologies. Their clients gain not only from access to more IT professionals with a wider span of technical knowledge and experience than an in-house IT department might be able to offer, but also from the introduction of structured methodologies and procedures.

Buying in IT services as and when required gives customers flexibility and the ability to increase or decrease capacity for application development and maintenance quickly and efficiently without the delays that are inherent in recruiting more staff (or redundancies/redeployment).

SOMERFIELD

The UK supermarket chain Somerfield decided to split its software development work between the UK and India following the success of a systems integration project undertaken by TCS. As reported in *Computer Weekly*, the project consolidated the number of different systems used by Somerfield, covering 300 applications, 900 interfaces, 4,000 batch jobs and 120 different databases. By using TCS to unify three different coding systems for stock items, which were stored in three different databases, Somerfield was able to save more than £1 million over in-house costs. TCS received fixed price payments linked to completion of significant milestones during the course of the project. While the development work was carried out in Kolkata (formerly Calcutta), specification and implementation tasks remained at Somerfield's head office in Bristol.

'TCS is at least as efficient as our internal IT team and 20 per cent cheaper than doing projects in-house,' said Tom Scott, Somerfield's IT director. 'By outsourcing finance, supply chain systems, process

> modelling, software testing, business intelligence and web-based projects, Somerfield hopes to keep IT costs low and improve overall business efficiency.'
>
> Price was not the only reason behind the decision to outsource to India. Access to specialist IT skills and flexibility were also important factors. Using TCS, Somerfield was able to double the size of its development team and increase flexibility without the need for more office space. To keep service levels high, Somerfield uses another Indian supplier, Zensar, for some projects, particularly benchmarking exercises.
>
> www.computerweekly.com

GREATER FOCUS ON CORE BUSINESS OBJECTIVES

Many of the IT systems used in organizations today are not differentiators and do not add competitive advantage. These are IT functions that are expected to work day in, day out and only become critical if they fail and are not promptly rectified, when they can consume a lot of management time and attention. They are not appreciated for the value they add to the organization's business nor do they move the organization forward into new markets or new products/services.

Some IT departments choose to outsource these functions so that the in-house staff can focus on strategic developments and supporting core business objectives. This has the added advantage of raising the status and profile of the in-house IT department. The focus moves away from operational problems and towards exploiting IT systems for the benefit of the organization.

> **FOXTONS**
>
> The London estate agency firm, Foxtons, has used offshore outsourcing to enable its in-house IT team to focus on systems integration, network support, system performance tuning and database management of core systems. LogicaCMG in the UK originally developed Microsoft-based customer relationship management and workflow applications for Foxtons and these were introduced in 2002. Further development and support of these systems has been outsourced to LogicaCMG's offshore facility in India, saving £40,000 to £50,000 annually.
>
> Having considered a number of offshore IT service companies, including some based in Russia and Eastern Europe, Foxtons decided to remain with LogicaCMG, using its offshore resources. 'The question people ask is how you manage the fear factor of outsourcing work offshore. We believe it's about getting the best quality for our money and giving our IT people the opportunity to work on more exciting projects,' Tim Carter, Foxton's IT director told *Computing*. 'It's given us the ability

> to be much more focused on quality and we can be more reactive to the requirements of the business.' Using the savings made by sending work offshore, Foxtons has restructured the in-house systems integration team and invested in further training for IT staff.
>
> www.computing.co.uk

PRODUCTIVITY AND SERVICE IMPROVEMENTS

Organizations can improve productivity and service levels by outsourcing IT services. This is not the only way to achieve these results, but the nature of the outsourcing process and the influence of working with a professional IT services company can bring added advantages.

Offshore companies tend to be very process driven and this leads the customer to become more process orientated and to define requirements precisely and accurately. During the transition phase, when responsibility for the IT function passes from the customer to the supplier, systems must be formally documented, which helps reduce the risk of depending on a small number of in-house individuals who may understand an IT system very well but may not, in the past, have passed that knowledge on to anyone else.

As part of the outsourcing process, the customer needs to examine service level requirements critically. This helps both customer and service provider to understand what is and what is not acceptable. Some organizations believe that poor performance can be confronted more quickly and effectively with an external outsourcing supplier. The contractual obligations of an outsourcing agreement mean that accountability is clearly defined and penalties can be imposed for poor performance.

Imaging technology is used extensively by offshore companies – moving paper documents such as invoices and orders between countries is simply inefficient, but scanning this material into a database that can be accessed in any country reduces paper flows and improves productivity. This technology is, of course, not new, but its implementation is rarely seen as top priority or expected to produce significant benefits on its own. Offshore outsourcing can tip the balance.

> ### NECTAR LOYALTY CARD
> To be ready for the launch of the Nectar loyalty card in September 2002, Loyalty Management UK needed an outsourcing supplier that could develop and support a new infrastructure in just over a year. *Computing* reported that the company wanted to use a supplier with global reach and decided to use Infosys, an Indian service provider. Nectar is now the

> largest loyalty programme in the UK. Infosys has also carried out an overhaul of the Nectar website, a major project that involved re-engineering call centre applications and a series of batch interfaces. 'At the start of the web-site re-launch, we had one Infosys technical project manager on site here and a business analyst. They worked with us on drawing up the specification, and that went through the design and build stage,' said Roger Sniezek, head of programme management. 'As we moved into the testing phase, specialists would come over to undertake functional and performance testing, and integration testing. We then moved over to the support team as we put everything live, getting documentation and hand-over ready. Part of that is done onshore, then the support gradually moves offshore.'
>
> www.computing.co.uk

BUSINESS TRANSFORMATION AND NEW DEVELOPMENTS

Major company reorganizations take time and effort and outsourcing can be used to support the change process. Internal politics, other new company initiatives and resistance to change can thwart business transformation. Outsourced services are less affected by these factors. One approach is to transfer responsibility for legacy system operation and maintenance to an outsourcing supplier while the in-house team focuses on the development and implementation of new systems.

Outsourcing can also be used selectively to introduce new technology or applications that require skills that, at least initially, are in short supply in-house. By outsourcing these activities to specialist companies, organizations can trial new technology without losing ground to their competitors and before committing to the expense of training in-house staff. Applications that prove to be commercially viable can be brought back in-house when the IT department has developed the appropriate skills base.

3 Risks and Countermeasures

Offshore sourcing does not always live up to the hype. The prospect of short-term cost savings may look very attractive, but we should not forget the disadvantages of offshoring that need to be addressed. These dangers, listed in Table 3.1, need to be considered as part of the initial decision to move work overseas and countermeasures put in place to mitigate the risks involved.

Offshoring needs to be placed within an overall sourcing strategy. Companies need to understand which processes are core to their business and provide competitive advantage and shareholder value. These are less likely to be suitable candidates for offshoring, especially if short-term financial gains lead to longer-term problems and a loss of competitive advantage. Although the offshore industry is maturing, projects still have to be fairly large to justify the risk and additional overhead expense of moving work overseas. For the time being at least, offshoring is unlikely to be a practical option for small companies or small-scale projects.

Offshore suppliers vary considerably in their maturity, experience and level of business knowledge. They are less likely than onshore service providers to have industry specific expertise or to understand how businesses work in the UK. Evaluating potential suppliers is made all the more difficult by the large number of suppliers and locations available. Lower cost countries do not always have the services that we take for granted in the UK. Electrical power supplies may not be constant or

Table 3.1 *Offshore sourcing risks*

Hidden costs
Cultural differences
Geopolitical instability
Difficult business environments
Intellectual property protection
Other legal concerns
Security and confidentiality issues
Data protection
Loss of technical expertise
Loss of business knowledge
Loss of flexibility and control
Customer backlash
Negative impact on IT professionals

reliable; severe weather can cause major disruption and telephone lines may be vulnerable to theft or damage.

HIDDEN COSTS

Risks

While low wage rates in offshore destinations suggest that dramatic savings can be made, the true costs of offshore sourcing can be much higher and offer only modest savings over retaining work onshore. Up-front costs are substantial and services may need to be closely monitored and refined for several years before they meet the customer's expectations. Costs increase because of the following factors:

- Onshore teams need cultural awareness training so that they can work effectively with the offshore team.
- Travel costs are high, as executives and managers need to travel regularly to the offshore destination.
- Telecommunications costs increase, especially if the offshore team is accessing mainframes or servers remotely.
- Onshore staff may have to work more overtime so that they can speak to colleagues in the offshore team who are working in a different time zone.
- Additional legal advice is needed to cope with the complexity of a contract that spans two or more countries and legislative systems.
- Managing an offshore contract is a more complex and onerous task than managing onshore outsourcing and, consequently, it is more costly.

Countermeasures

Companies considering different sourcing options for IT services need to look beyond the up-front cost savings on wages to review the total cost of services moved overseas and compare this with the cost of in-house services or onshore outsourcing. Anyone preparing to send work offshore needs to ensure that the whole organization is ready for the change – senior executive sponsorship is in place, communication plans developed, contract management structure set up and fully staffed, training programmes organized and so on.

CULTURAL DIFFERENCES

Risks

Offshore sourcing brings together people who view the world from very different perspectives, with different historical contexts from which they view the present, and different expectations about working relationships and norms. The most obvious difference is language and good English skills are clearly important for any offshore supplier offering services to UK companies. But communication depends on more than written or spoken words. Accents, the use of colloquialisms and body language all contribute or detract from our understanding of each other. People from different cultural backgrounds can cause confusion or misunderstanding quite inadvertently.

Social and business etiquette varies between countries. Greetings, forms of address, gestures, value systems and concepts of punctuality differ around the world. It is easy to cause offence or give the impression that you are inefficient; or to get frustrated if you do not understand your offshore supplier's culture and way of doing business. This can quickly lead to a breakdown in the relationship from which it is difficult to recover.

In the UK we are used to questioning authority, challenging our managers if we disagree with their ideas and putting forward our own suggestions. In many non-European cultures, employees are reluctant to say 'no' or to question the customer's instructions, even if the offshore organization has a better way of doing things. During meetings in the UK, managers will commonly pursue a discussion to its logical conclusion and then clarify a number of action points. In some offshore countries, once they have understood the point being made, the team will abruptly change the subject since they see no further need for discussion.

The larger the distance between the onshore and offshore teams, the more difficult and time-consuming it becomes to organize regular face-to-face meetings and interaction. Long journeys can be expensive and tiring and travel in developing countries can be a problem. Different time zones may make it difficult to find a suitable time for team members to speak by telephone or hold a videoconference. One solution might be to send a UK manager to work with the offshore team, but this can be an expensive option that eats into potential savings.

Even within the UK, company cultures vary. Some organizations have embraced outsourcing as an efficient way of buying in services, freeing up IT professionals to focus on exploiting IT for competitive advantage. Other companies believe that they can only ensure proper control and maintain service levels if IT functions are operated by the in-house team. If companies with these two different value systems merge, the resulting culture clash is likely to cause disruption and angst. As some outsourcing suppliers have found to their cost, even successful contracts can be terminated if the culture within their client's organization shifts significantly.

Countermeasures

Any team working with others in another country can benefit from training to enhance cultural awareness and understanding. However effective a UK-based account manager might be, it is very important that in-house business analysts and managers visit the offshore team. Managers should ideally visit every two or three months to walk the job, talk about objectives and priorities and get to know the offshore team. The offshore team serving UK customers will be strengthened if it includes one or more people who have had work experience in the USA or Europe.

A company relatively new to offshoring would be advised to send only the more technical, tightly specified pieces of work overseas until they are confident that an effective working relationship has been developed. Loosely defined requirements that require a lot of interaction between developers and users are more likely to suffer from communication problems caused by cultural differences. Given the difficulties caused by cultural clashes, some organizations prefer to use near-shore locations to minimize communication difficulties and time differences. UK companies may be drawn to Ireland or Eastern Europe, though in terms of language India, the Philippines and South Africa also offer advantages.

TIETOENATOR

The Norwegian branch of European IT services company TietoEnator decided in 2001 to outsource a human resources and payroll system project to Arcadia, a small company in St Petersburg that employs about 100 developers. The system supports several thousand end users, was written with Borland Software's Delphi 3 and was to be updated using Delphi 6 and Microsoft's SQL Server. A number of mistakes on both sides, mainly in communication, led to the project being a year behind its original six-month schedule.

TietoEnator chose a Russian company because other Scandinavian companies were too expensive and India seemed too far away. In retrospect, Arcadia recognized that they were so excited about the prospect of winning a contract from a large western client that they underestimated the cost of the project and overestimated their ability to complete it. Problems emerged soon after the project started. The software that Arcadia was given to work on had a number of bugs and all the software documentation was in Norwegian. When the project was nearly due, the Russian team still had not found a way to implement a significant number of important features in the programme.

The project was the subject of a case study at the computer science department of the University of Oslo, as reported in *Computerworld*. Veger Imsland, author of the case study, has reported that the first problems emerged in project initiation: Arcadia's inadequate domain knowledge was ignored, TietoEnator failed to transfer the required knowledge to Arcadia and both sides underestimated the resources required for the project. Neither company paid enough attention to the project once it started, nor did they double-check the weekly status reports that indicated everything was going well. Not one face-to-face meeting was held in the first six months of the project and misunderstandings were frequent because employees were not communicating in

> their native languages. Project managers on both sides faced information overload because they were responsible for all communications between the companies.
>
> www.computerworld.com

GEOPOLITICAL INSTABILITY AND DIFFICULT BUSINESS ENVIRONMENTS

Risks

Regardless of the competence or competitiveness of an offshore service provider, geopolitical concerns or social unrest can pose major risks for any organization considering offshore working. War, terrorism, political conflict or religious strife present major disadvantages to any offshore market. Each part of the world has its own risks – in the UK we too have experience of the disruption and damage caused by terrorism. So, in considering the stability of any offshore location, a judgement needs to be made about the degree of risk.

Since India holds the major share of the offshore market, the geopolitical risk most frequently mentioned is the dispute between Pakistan and India over Kashmir. Since both countries are nuclear powers, any military conflict between the two nations could have very serious implications for Indian businesses. Venezuela illustrates the damage that can be caused by instability. The country was emerging as a potential offshore location until social unrest greatly diminished its prospects of developing a successful global IT services industry. Companies run the risk of becoming locked into a particular country that is stable now but descends into unrest in future years.

Other political and business issues include taxes, inadequate infrastructure, unreliable power supplies, inefficient dispute resolution through the local legal system, restrictive regulations covering business start-ups and poor protection for personal data and intellectual property. The cost of offshore services is at risk from exchange-rate fluctuations and salary inflation at the offshore location. Any of these factors can be problematic. India's legal system is generally regarded as overly bureaucratic and slow, and organizations buying services from Indian suppliers often look for contract enforcement outside of India so that disputes can be resolved without lengthy delays. China has a poor reputation for protection of copyright and intellectual property, based, in part, on the country's attitude towards pirated software.

Countermeasures

Any company contemplating offshore sourcing needs to assess the risks associated with various locations. Different countries have different technical strengths, so the evaluation of sourcing options needs to balance the strengths of the IT services industry in a specific country against the geopolitical risks. Three potential countermeasures can be adopted to mitigate these risks:

- IT services can be sourced from near-shore locations, which have more stable economies and share common approaches to business regulation. In the UK this might mean choosing Ireland or Eastern Europe in preference to Asia.
- A multinational service provider that operates from a number of different locations can be chosen. This gives the customer the option of exploiting the best location for different IT functions or services safe in the knowledge that if political or social problems arise, work can be transferred to another location with the same provider.
- A company can choose to source IT services from several different locations, avoiding the risk of becoming over-dependent on one country.

A strong and vibrant trade association can help overcome many of the problems associated with a particular country by supporting the development of the offshore industry and lobbying the government to improve the business environment. NASSCOM in India is a great example of an influential and effective trade organization.

Some governments establish technology parks that provide reliable telecommunications links and network facilities. Problems caused by inadequate electricity supply can be overcome using dedicated generators and back-up facilities. All organizations sending work offshore should have contingency plans in place so that they can move work to an alternative site should a disaster strike their offshore location.

For some companies, commercial interests override concerns about geopolitical risks. Any company wanting to develop its market in a specific country may set up an offshore centre to build up local experience and contacts. Hence some software companies who see the potential for market growth in China have set up development centres there. Any risks associated with doing business in China are accepted in the interests of the future possibility of developing new markets.

LEGAL ISSUES – INCLUDING INTELLECTUAL PROPERTY PROTECTION

Risks

Establishing a sound contractual basis for offshore services is made all the more difficult by the complexity of working with different legislative systems and the challenge of negotiating with distant managers. Legal advice is also more expensive, as specialist skills are required and there is more work to do.

One of the key concerns in offshore contracts is the protection of intellectual property. Companies need to determine the degree to which the intellectual property they move offshore, or is developed on their behalf offshore, is protected in the local courts. Many of the countries providing offshore services do not offer the same level of protection for intellectual property as is found in Western Europe and the USA.

Countries that are members of the World Trade Organization and adhere to the intellectual property provisions known as TRIPS (Trade-Related Aspects of Intellectual Property rightS) should offer adequate protection, but this depends on local enforcement. Attitudes towards trade theft vary – a country's record on protecting film and music copyright and fighting software piracy is a good indicator.

Rachel Burnett, a solicitor who specializes in IT and outsourcing advice and contracts told me:

> If there is an infringement of IPR [intellectual property rights] used by the offshore outsourcing service provider, the immediate and best recourse will be in the first instance against the provider for *breach of contract*, because the provider will be in breach of contract if there are the normal obligations in respect of IPR protection in the contract. Ideally (generally speaking and in most cases) the contract would be subject to the law and jurisdiction of the client's jurisdiction. I would emphasize the importance of the contract.

Countermeasures

The outsourcing contract is an important risk management tool. Effective issue management and dispute resolution processes, incorporated into the contract, help both parties find solutions to problems relatively quickly and inexpensively. This stops small difficulties escalating into major issues. By defining rights and responsibilities when the agreement terminates, the contract provides a helpful framework at what can be a difficult time. Offshore services need to be more tightly defined and contracts more prescriptive to cover the risks involved in managing an operation in a foreign jurisdiction.

Rachel Burnett advised me:

> The main legal issue is to have a good enforceable contract and, as part of that, careful consideration needs to be given to defining the jurisdiction for interpretation and enforcement of that contract. Dispute management is also important, for example the parties should perhaps at least consider arbitration in the event of a dispute, which can be a useful alternative to courts for parties in different jurisdictions rather than local courts in either party's jurisdiction.

Once the contract is signed, the customer needs to monitor performance and compliance with agreed service levels. Regular audits, back-up procedure reviews and an actively managed change control process all help to identify potential problems for resolution before they escalate into major concerns.

The best way to protect intellectual property is to detail the supplier's particular obligations in the contract. Clients can also:

- Require their suppliers to avoid providing services to their client's competitors or to have demonstrable procedures in place to segregate the services provided to the different organizations. This segregation of services might also be required to protect confidentiality.
- Prohibit their suppliers from outsourcing work to a third party, at least without prior approval.

Source code may be lost or misused inadvertently by the offshore supplier's employees or may be deliberately stolen by dishonest staff or taken by disgruntled employees when they leave the supplier. A number of measures can be adopted to cover these risks:

- The offshore supplier should have rigorous procedures in place to protect source code from being lost, for example by preventing employees transferring code onto PCs to work at home or bringing laptops or notebook PCs from home into work.
- The supplier should thoroughly vet new recruits, confirming information given on CVs and carrying out background checks.
- The stability of the supplier's workforce is a useful indicator of job satisfaction within the company. There is strong competition between offshore suppliers for the best IT professionals and managers, so some movement between companies is to be expected. But customers should be wary of higher than average attrition rates or any unexpected fluctuations. They should review the supplier's personnel policies and career development schemes. Employees who are well treated are less likely to be sufficiently dissatisfied to want to damage their employer by stealing trade property.

SECURITY, CONFIDENTIALITY AND DATA PROTECTION

Risks

In any outsourcing relationship, the supplier has access to information and other assets that the customer would normally regard as confidential. Risks include a loss of control of physical and electronic security, especially where processing takes place in another country. How will this be monitored and managed? Who will be allowed access? What are the procedures when there has been a breach of security? Who will audit the security processes?

Data protection is a key issue. The UK's Data Protection Act 1998 places obligations on UK organizations to handle personal data with care. In this context, personal data is defined as data held about living, identifiable individuals. Data users have formally to notify the Information Commissioner, and enter the details in a public register. They must follow the principles set out in the legislation to ensure that personal data is held, processed and used properly, fairly and lawfully and that there are adequate procedures in place for keeping it secure.

Rachel Burnett advised me:

> Data protection will be relevant only if personal data is part of the outsourcing. What is particularly important about data protection in an offshore outsourcing context is the eighth Data Protection Principle, which states: 'Personal data shall not be transferred to a country or territory outside the European Economic Area unless that country or territory ensures an adequate level of protection for the rights and freedoms of data subjects in relation to the processing of personal data.'
>
> Some countries outside the EEA have been approved by the European Commission as having adequate data protection laws, e.g. Hungary and Switzerland. There is a voluntary self-certification scheme in the US, the 'Safe Harbour' scheme, and companies committing to that also have an adequate level of protection. An 'adequate level of protection' is one which is adequate in all the circumstances of the case, taking account of such matters as the nature of the personal data, the country or territory to which the data are to be transferred, the purposes for which and the period during which the data are intended to be processed, the law in force in the country or territory in question, its international obligations, any relevant codes of conduct or other rules which are enforceable there, and any security measures taken in respect of the data there.
>
> There are exceptions to the Principle, e.g. the transfer is necessary for the performance of a contract involving or for the benefit of the data subject. Or, the transfer is made on terms of an approved kind, which ensure adequate safeguards for the rights and freedoms of data subjects. There is a set of model clauses for controller-to-controller transfers approved by the European Commission. These clauses may therefore be adopted or equivalent provisions may be drafted as contractual limitations taking the particular needs into account in the outsourcing contract itself.

Countermeasures

Before moving any work offshore, an organization needs to understand and document its security and privacy requirements. A security evaluation of the supplier's policies and procedures can then be carried out before any contract is signed.

Secure infrastructure is a basic building block of an offshore service and the supplier is responsible for establishing and maintaining network security policies, statements and procedures. The offshore service provider also needs to have in place physical security measures, such as access control, to ensure that only authorized personnel enter customer service areas. Offshore agreements should include an accountability/ownership framework so that customer and supplier have clear roles and responsibilities and security is assured at an appropriate level. Regular audits and penetration tests will ensure that standards are maintained.

Suppliers should have security processes in place that comply with internationally recognized standards such as BS 7799. The security products used should have been tested independently of the manufacturer and awarded certification to IT Security Evaluation Criteria (ITSEC) or Common Criteria (CC) standards (equivalent to ISO 15408). Suppliers should also employ qualified security professionals who meet recognized standards such as the Certified Information System Security Professional (CISSP) exam, which is administered by the International Information Systems Certification Consortium, based in Florida.

The Software Engineering Institute has developed the Team Software Process (TSP) to improve software quality and security. Specific code modules are traceable to individual programmers. Within TSP, software engineers are trained to follow high-quality development practices. The focus is on design, requirements, analysis and code review before testing. The team knows who owns what code. The process is useful for identifying and fixing defects as well as finding security vulnerabilities. Because code can be traced back to individual programmers, TSP offers greater scope than other security standards for combating hidden malware that can be inserted in software developed anywhere in the world (visit www.sei.cmu.edu/tsp for further information about TSP).

Information protection needs to be designed to meet the customer's requirements and the different categories of information used. Personal data must be protected in accordance with EU regulations. As a general rule it is preferable to maintain personal data in systems based onshore and allow restricted access to this data from overseas. Encrypting the data; or creating test data with sensitive information removed; or disabling functions that would allow data to be copied can give further protection. All workstations at the offshore supplier should have disabled CD and floppy disk drives to help prevent wrongful data transfer. Employees should have secure workspaces including secure storage space.

METROPOLITAN POLICE

In February 2004 the UK Metropolitan Police announced that it was looking for a new outsourcing supplier to consolidate three existing contracts in a deal that could be worth £650 million. The services to be outsourced include core IT and communications systems, including the development, supply and support of infrastructure, desktop, network and possibly software services. The contract is likely to start in July 2005 and will last 10 years, with a possible extension to 13 years. The contract is unlikely to be awarded to an offshore supplier. 'We're looking at tying

> together our systems because we believe it would result in better value for money,' said a spokeswoman for the Metropolitan Police. 'We have to consider all the proposals coming in, but I don't believe we'll be awarding the contract to an offshore company. The criteria for us to go offshore are extremely stringent and it is unlikely that any company will meet these.'
>
> www.computing.co.uk

LOSS OF TECHNICAL EXPERTISE AND BUSINESS KNOWLEDGE

Risks

Many of the applications and services that might be provided by offshore suppliers in the future are currently maintained and operated by onshore experienced IT professionals. When work is moved offshore, these staff must share their knowledge of systems and business processes with the offshore team. Once this is completed the in-house IT staff will either move to new roles or leave the organization.

Unless carefully managed there is a risk that the organization sending work offshore will lose technical expertise that is hard to replace and an understanding of the company that may not be readily apparent. Valuable knowledge may cover a number of areas:

- organizational knowledge about how IT products, services and systems are combined to support business objectives;
- an understanding of company culture and how this influences IT decision-making;
- social networks within the organization that help IT projects to achieve results;
- strategic knowledge about the competitive advantages gained through IT;
- business sector knowledge about competitor organizations, their processes and use of IT.

Once work is moved offshore, detailed knowledge of applications and services will only be found overseas and this makes it very hard to bring work back to the UK. Without relevant technical expertise, the organization will also find it difficult to monitor and manage the quality of service delivered by the offshore team. This can leave companies vulnerable to poor service and inflated prices.

Companies outsourcing work within the UK have the advantage that current IT staff can transfer to the service provider. If a later decision is made to return work in-house, IT staff may transfer back from the supplier. Clearly it is not possible when work moves offshore for employees to move between organizations in this way.

The effect of offshore sourcing on the IT department will also influence the future recruitment of IT professionals. The organization may be seen as undervaluing the contribution of in-house IT staff and of having only limited opportunities for interesting technical work. It will then be more difficult to attract professionals with the level of skills and expertise needed to develop IT strategy, exploit technology to meet business aims and explore the use of new technologies. The position will be all the more acute when the economy improves and IT skills are in more limited supply.

Countermeasures

At an early stage in the planning process, companies need to identify the skills and knowledge they need to retain when work is moved offshore and the people that might meet these requirements. Many organizations choose to retain business-critical functions and user-facing roles, such as application design and integration, user-facing process management, IT architecture and information management.

A number of new roles need to be introduced to manage the offshore relationship and monitor the services provided – contract management, relationship management, change control, contract administration, budget management and so on. IT professionals who understand both the systems being developed offshore and the client company's culture and processes make excellent candidates for these new roles. Training in relationship development, contract law, negotiation and other relevant topics needs to be organized, preferably before work is moved overseas.

> **DELL**
>
> Along with many other US-based IT suppliers, Dell shifted technical support to centres in India and elsewhere. But complaints about the quality of technical support led to the company moving support for its Optiplex desktops and Latitude notebooks back to US call centres, including those in Texas, Idaho and Tennessee. 'Corporate customers were telling us they didn't like the level of support they were getting, and in the normal course of business, we made some adjustments,' Jon Weisblatt, a Dell spokesman, told *Computerworld*. Support calls for other products, as well as consumer support, continue to be handled on the basis of capacity at Dell's 20 global call centres.
>
> www.computerworld.com

LOSS OF FLEXIBILITY AND CONTROL

Risks

Services defined at the outset are covered by contract, but what about new services and changed requirements that develop at a later stage? Internal UK-based IT departments are under the direct control of the organization's senior management, but it is much harder to develop an effective working relationship with a team based in another country, in a different time zone. It is more difficult to spot potential problems and to keep projects on track. Service and requirement changes have to be defined and specified in detail, then negotiated and agreed with the supplier. How can an organization be confident that its needs and priorities will be recognized and adopted by the offshore team?

A common complaint is that some offshore firms lack business knowledge and this becomes more significant as they take on more complex IT projects. As a result, project timescales and costs are underestimated and systems fail to meet business requirements. Offshore sourcing is least successful when business processes change frequently and rapid system evolution is required – and more appropriate for maintaining and modifying legacy systems, where changes can be tightly specified and scheduled at a somewhat slower pace.

Countermeasures

A formal methodology is essential to ensure proper control over a project or function being carried out by an offshore team. This provides a framework for communications between onshore and offshore team members. Standard planning, monitoring and risk management techniques also need to be adopted. Experienced service providers have well-developed methodologies, but smaller, specialist suppliers may be less well organized. In both cases, the customer needs to make sure that appropriate processes are in place to match business requirements.

Unambiguous and comprehensive written requirements are another vital component. Delivery dates for project products need to be agreed and documented. Offshore teams may have different expectations and will want to be directed – so do not make any assumptions or take any project requirements for granted. Document and agree everything.

Companies new to offshoring are strongly advised to test the approach on small, non-critical projects and gradually build up the amount of work sent offshore. As experience and familiarity grow, a more informed judgement can be made about the potential loss of flexibility and control over an offshore team.

WASHINGTON STATE HEALTH CARE AGENCY

Dramatic savings promised by offshoring can only be delivered for well-defined, stable requirements. When the Washington State Health Care Agency received bids for the development of a new insurance benefits administration system, the proposal to use offshore workers was the only bid to come in under the £2 million budget set by the state legislature.

> Texas-based prime contractor Healthaxis, working with Indian outsourcer Satyam Computer Services, submitted the winning bid. The savings came mainly from reduced salary costs. Healthaxis listed programmer rates at £19 per hour, but other bidders rates started at £100.
>
> The new system was initially expected to be in place by the end of June 2003, but, as reported in *Computerworld*, this slipped to June 2004. Problems included testing, design quality and usability. Both the healthcare agency and supplier had difficulties with the system requirements that were not apparent at the outset. The project scope was larger than at first anticipated. The delay cost the healthcare agency about £784,000 in maintenance and support costs for running its health benefits' applications on a system hosted by another state agency.
>
> Drawing lessons learned from the project, the healthcare agency's IT manager, Tom Neitzel, said, 'I would be certain that clear requirements, written requirements, are developed and agreed upon. Make sure that clear deliverable dates are documented and agreed upon by all. Assume nothing. That is what I am learning here, and it is being reinforced.'
>
> www.computerworld.com

CUSTOMER BACKLASH

Risks

Recent media reports of the offshoring trend have focused public attention on the number of jobs 'lost' to overseas workers and have highlighted service problems. Bad news travels fast and poor experiences with offshore working are no exception. At its worst, offshoring is seen as an evil curse, imposed by fat cat company executives on a downtrodden workforce.

This stereotype can influence public opinion and the perception of low-cost and poor-quality customer service can damage a company's reputation and discourage potential customers. Any company considering moving work offshore has to consider the possibility that customer-facing services will deteriorate, even temporarily, resulting in a harmful backlash. Good news stories about service improvements will not be widely reported, but the media spotlight will fall on any trouble spots.

Countermeasures

Organizations should pay particular attention to customer-facing services and put in place robust contingency measures to tackle any unforeseen problems. Customer complaints should be closely monitored during the introduction of offshore working and any increases or trends reviewed in detail so that remedial action can be taken before issues escalate into highly visible service disruptions.

INDIANA DEPARTMENT OF WORKFORCE DEVELOPMENT

Some offshore projects have been stalled by political pressure. The state of Indiana cancelled a £8.5 million IT development contract with supplier TCS America that would have seen up to 65 contract workers from India moved onto the project. TCS America won the contract with a bid that was £4.5 million lower than the proposal submitted by the nearest competitor. No Indiana-based firms bid for the contract. The project would have replaced a mainframe tax and unemployment claims processing system with a client/server system written in Java. The Indian contract staff would have worked alongside 18 state employees in the Indiana Government Centre.

Governor Joe Kernan ordered the Indiana Department of Workforce Development (DWD) to cancel the contract as part of a new initiative called Opportunity Indiana. A statement issued by Kernan said, 'After having a chance to discuss our vision of how the state should do business, and how we can provide better opportunities to Indiana companies and workers, we concluded that this contract did not fit in that framework.'

www.computerworld.com

NEGATIVE IMPACT ON IT PROFESSIONALS

Risks

Unless it is well managed, any move to carry out work overseas creates anxiety about job security and concern about future prospects. A poorly planned offshore programme can lead to a loss of valuable talent and expertise within the organization. IT professionals may feel under threat and unwanted. The situation is made worse by a period of uncertainty. Once an offshore project is launched, several months are likely to pass before the supplier and location are finally chosen and the impact on in-house IT professionals becomes fully apparent. Not knowing what the future holds can be the most demoralizing and demotivating factor and can lead to falling standards of performance, increased sickness and difficulty in attracting new talent.

When work is outsourced within the UK, the Transfer of Undertakings (Protection of Employment) Regulations, or TUPE, guarantee staff employment under existing terms with the service provider. Organizations must consult their employees in good time before any transfer of their employment to the supplier takes place. If IT functions move offshore, some employees may face redundancy. Where an employer proposes to make 20 or more employees redundant at a business site within three months, employees have the right to be consulted via trade unions or employee representatives at least one month before the first of the dismissals occurs. The financial compensation for inadequate consultation by the employer is up to 90 days pay.

During the planning and transition process, some IT staff may decide to leave and pursue their careers elsewhere and this can increase the pressure on those that stay. Employees with experience of company systems and knowledge about business processes are needed in the transition phase to train the offshore workers.

Countermeasures

All employees closely watch the way in which an organization handles the need to redeploy staff or make some people redundant. Are senior executives open and honest? Do they value their employees? How hard does the company try to find alternative roles for those displaced by offshore sourcing? Is the company prepared to invest in retraining and coaching for those forced to look for alternative employment? Whatever might appear in the company's mission statement or annual report, the organization's true aims and values are visible to all at this time. This can influence much wider issues than the offshore IT project – the organization's reputation in the job market, its relationship with the local community, the views of shareholders and the likely success of future business change programmes.

There are a number of actions that can be taken to support and encourage those IT staff affected by the offshore programme:

- Create a realistic transition plan with clear timescales and milestones. Identify those points at which, as work packages are completed, specific groups of staff will be released for redeployment or redundancy.
- Clarify the options that are available to staff displaced by offshoring as soon as possible to give time for people to reflect on their possible future career paths.
- Offer retraining and help for those seeking new employment or looking to set up their own companies.
- Consider paying bonuses in addition to redundancy packages to those staff that are needed to train the offshore team during the transition stage.
- Give employees as much notice as possible about the changes that will be made.
- Issue regular reports about the progress made in the offshore project.
- Remember that face-to-face communication is very important at this time – bad news should be given in person, not in a written communication.
- Start formal meetings with trade unions or other staff representatives at an early stage. Be prepared to justify the decision to move work offshore. Clarify whether each topic discussed is open for consultation or simply an opportunity for management to inform the unions what

will happen. Naturally trade unions will push for as much consultation as possible, but will be angered by a false assurance about a consultative process.

4 Managing Offshore Outsourcing Projects

If done well, offshore outsourcing can produce significant savings, but if poorly managed the costs of resolving difficulties and getting an offshore project back on track can wipe out virtually all anticipated benefits. Many organizations today are experimenting with offshore outsourcing for small, non-critical projects so that they can develop their expertise and be well placed to be more competitive in the future by fully exploiting the global IT services market.

In this chapter we look at how organizations should tackle offshore projects, from inception through to implementation. Many of the guidelines and best practices apply equally to onshore and offshore outsourcing but there are some significant differences:

- Moving offshore requires knowledge of the relative strengths and weaknesses of the IT services market in different countries, the local business environment and geopolitical risks, as well as an understanding of the individual outsourcing suppliers.

- The development of the global market has produced many different business models that can be adopted; for example companies may choose to go with established outsourcing players with global development centres or major offshore companies, or new offshore suppliers with a head office in the UK.

- Due diligence has to be more wide ranging and thorough. You are dealing with an unfamiliar business environment and should take nothing for granted.

- In onshore outsourcing deals, staff would expect to transfer to become employees of the service provider. Offshore contracts often result in redeployment or redundancy.

- The transfer of knowledge about systems and business processes is one of the major challenges in implementing offshore services. The offshore team is usually starting from scratch, learning about the client's business and systems.

Organizations with little or no experience of working overseas will find that they need new skills and expertise. Remember that suppliers are constantly preparing proposals, submitting bids and negotiating deals. These are core business activities for suppliers and they will employ the necessary specialists. Take care not to be put at a disadvantage as a potential client. Consider how your company's personnel, legal and purchasing departments can help in the offshore programme. If you need to appoint expert advisors, make sure that they are independent and impartial, with no vested interests. Advisors are an expensive resource, so ensure that:

- Their credentials are checked and their knowledge and depth of expertise are tested.
- Their role is clearly documented and explained to everyone working on the offshore project – advisors cannot make decisions for your organization.
- The external advisors are properly managed and remain focused only on their assigned roles.

Figure 4.1 illustrates the nine steps that form the outsourcing process.

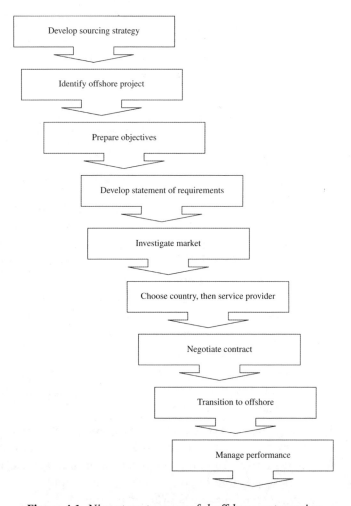

Figure 4.1 *Nine steps to successful offshore outsourcing*

SOURCING STRATEGY

The decision to move any IT project or service offshore should be made within the framework of an overall sourcing strategy. Any organization in the UK today is faced by an almost bewildering array of technologies, suppliers and business models. An effective sourcing strategy identifies the most profitable way to supply different IT services, taking account of corporate priorities and culture. The key elements of a sourcing strategy are illustrated in Figure 4.2.

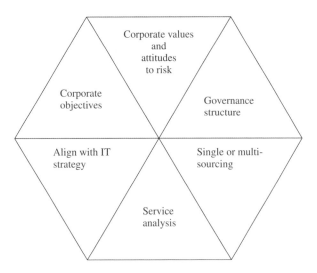

Figure 4.2 *Sourcing strategy*

Corporate objectives

The strategy should reflect your organization's aims and targets for current and future business prospects. Products and services that give your company competitive advantage may suggest IT functions that need to be kept in-house. Future business plans may indicate new technical skills that will be required and the strategy should show whether these are best acquired from external suppliers or developed in-house. Major business development plans may require additional resources temporarily and these projects may be outsourced.

Corporate values and attitudes to risk

Some organizations have deep-seated beliefs about outsourcing, either supporting the theory that proper control and flexibility can only be achieved by retaining all IT functions in-house or believing that a company should only carry out core functions and outsource as many activities as possible to derive maximum efficiencies and gain access to the widest range of technical skills.

Companies also have different attitudes to risk. Those that are risk-averse will want to outsource only to well-established suppliers. Multi-national companies are much more likely to be confident in working overseas and might already have contacts and insights into the countries where IT services industries are emerging.

Analysis of IT services

Current and future IT service requirements need to be analysed to indicate preferred methods of supply:

- IT functions that are to remain in-house;
- IT functions that are to be developed in conjunction with others;
  - joint ventures with service providers;
  - shared services with other organizations in the same business sector;
- possible candidates for outsourcing.

In determining which service falls into which category, three key factors need to be considered:

- **The degree to which the service offers competitive advantage:** Some IT functions win no words of congratulation from business users. Like the electricity or water supply, they are just expected to be available, with levels of service that are reliable and consistent. It makes little sense to invest a great deal of time and effort in these services making incremental improvements. They offer no competitive advantage and make good candidates for outsourcing. A supplier with relevant expertise can apply lessons learned elsewhere to drive through economies and efficiencies.

- **The technical expertise that is available in the IT department:** If new skills are required to develop systems for competitive advantage, legacy system maintenance and operation can be outsourced, leaving spare capacity so that the in-house team can develop the new technical skills required, Alternatively, if the application development is outsourced to achieve speedy results, arrangements should be made to transfer knowledge back to the in-house team so that they can take responsibility for the system as soon as practical. Where new skills are required, for example to support new regulatory requirements that apply to everyone in a business sector, a more effective approach might be to set-up a shared service centre.

- **The track record and maturity of the IT services industry, which varies between countries and across the different IT functions:** Where a number of well-qualified and experienced suppliers compete for business, it makes sense to investigate the possibility of outsourcing to achieve economies and free up internal resources for other projects. Global organizations may want to exploit the technical strengths of particular countries by setting up local IT organizations.

Multi-sourcing

One of the key decisions to be made is the choice between:

- a single or limited number of suppliers, possibly a prime contractor who subcontracts work to specialist companies as necessary; or
- multiple suppliers, perhaps a catalogue of preferred suppliers.

Both approaches have been successfully adopted and both have the potential to cause problems as illustrated in Table 4.1.

Table 4.1 *Advantages and disadvantages of single- or multi-sourcing (derived from Cullen and Willcocks, 2003)*

Method of supply	Advantages	Disadvantages
Single or limited number of suppliers	1. Creates opportunity for investing in a deep, long-term relationship with supplier. 2. Easier to manage. 3. Performance measures can encompass services from beginning to end. 4. Easier to set-up user contact points for service queries. 5. Same standards and methodologies will be applied across all services.	1. Over-dependence on a limited number of suppliers. 2. Can be difficult to move to a new supplier if services deteriorate significantly. 3. Have to depend on main supplier bringing in specialist skills when required. 4. Limited competitive levers once contract signed.
Multiple suppliers	1. Reduced dependency on any one supplier. 2. Greater flexibility in choice of supplier. 3. Opportunity to use specialist suppliers who can offer focused expertise. 4. Opportunity to use different suppliers in different countries to meet local needs. 5. Maintains a degree of competition between suppliers. 6. Facilitates benchmarking.	1. Suppliers should be based in different countries to reduce geopolitical risks. 2. Potential for clashes and disagreement between suppliers. 3. More time-consuming and complex to manage. 4. Difficult to devise performance measures that show how well suppliers are working together. 5. Can be confusing for users. 6. Suppliers may adopt different methodologies and processes.

Service level agreements need to be developed for each outsourcing relationship. Where multiple suppliers are chosen, one service provider can be adopted as the lead supplier, responsible for coordinating the activities of all suppliers, operating the help desk and reporting on performance. An alternative approach is to structure the outsourcing deals in such a way that the suppliers are mutually dependent on each other. All suppliers should be required to implement the same methodologies and processes for project management, planning, change control and testing. These will form part of the service level agreement with each supplier.

Align with IT strategy

The sourcing strategy should support implementation of the corporate IT strategy in areas such as technical architecture, data storage strategy, leading edge technology adoption, application software upgrades, enterprise resource planning systems and quality management initiatives. It should also recognize the need to comply with all IT standards and policies including corporate project management standards, security policies and corporate business continuity plans.

Governance structures

The sourcing strategy should include a definition of the arrangements for monitoring implementation of the strategy, reviewing progress and agreeing modifications as the global IT services market develops and business imperatives change. The governance structure needs to include representatives from the purchasing and finance departments and must have authority over all significant IT service purchases wherever they originate. Without this corporate management, IT services may be purchased in a piecemeal fashion with little or no regard to system interfaces and future requirements, uncertain service boundaries between suppliers and a lack of clarity about performance indicators and user support services.

IDENTIFYING WHAT TO SOURCE OFFSHORE

Having decided to outsource an IT service, you need to determine the extent to which you will use offshore resources. To get the best results, you must think about this in terms of devising a global delivery model that combines onshore, near-shore and far-shore to best effect. A number of factors are used to determine which activities can profitably be carried out offshore:

- **Specificity and clarity of the requirements:** Offshore projects work best where there is no ambiguity or confusion about what is required. You need to be able to document requirements in detail and to get sign-off from all interested parties. The written record of requirements is all-important when the project team is working at a distance. Do not use offshore if you anticipate that a lot of clarification will be needed or if the project calls for interactive development.

- **User interaction:** Clearly an offshore team cannot have frequent face-to-face meetings with users. This makes consultation and discussion with users during the project largely impractical. Offshore working is more effective when there is only a limited need to involve users during the life of the project.

- **Sensitive and confidential data:** If this information is to be stored overseas or accessed remotely, you need to be sure that you can put adequate safeguards in place.

- **System integration:** Applications that are largely self-contained make the best offshore candidates.

- **Application life cycle:** Any application developed offshore needs to remain operational for about a year to justify the initial overheads and ensure an adequate return.

- **Project visibility:** Choosing offshore projects that have little impact outside your organization reduces the risk of any negative publicity. These projects can be used as opportunities for developing best practice and learning the lessons of how to tackle offshore projects without jeopardizing your organization's reputation.

- **Knowledge transfer:** When an offshore project is initiated the offshore team needs to learn more about your company, relevant business processes and the service requirements. If this information is readily available and well documented, knowledge can be shared efficiently and quickly with the offshore team.

- **Staff responses:** Job satisfaction and security are important factors for most of us. Companies beginning to trial offshore working should consider the well-being and future of their IT staff. A vibrant, innovative and well-motivated IT department will be critical to future business prosperity. Any decision to move work offshore should be well justified and transparent. Careful consideration needs to be given to the opportunities for alternative employment that can be offered to anyone who loses their job through offshore outsourcing.

- **Team size:** The significant cost advantages of offshore outsourcing are based on wage differentials and projects that need only a small team (say 10 staff or less) are unlikely to offer enough benefit to justify the risk and expense of moving work offshore. Service providers often offer discounts for larger numbers of staff so that projects with 50 or more people working offshore usually give the best savings ratios.

- **Hardware and software:** Offshore projects should have simple hardware and software requirements. At least initially, it is best to avoid offshore projects that would require your organization to buy duplicate or additional hardware at the offshore development centre and there should be only limited impact on software licensing costs.

- **Application environment:** Make sure that the technical skills you need in the overseas team are readily available in your chosen offshore location.
- **Large backlog of application problems:** Any application that has been running for a number of years is likely to have a number of outstanding problems and inadequacies that have not been addressed because of competing priorities or insufficient return for the cost of modifying the system. Moving this work offshore is an opportunity to bring new resources to the task and to implement changes cost-effectively.
- **Volatile requirements:** Choose projects with relatively stable requirements. If the project is constantly evolving, the offshore team will need to check out and confirm what is needed frequently and this is much harder working at a distance.

OBJECTIVES

Every project needs clear objectives. Make sure at the outset that your organization has defined what it wants to achieve and how it will know when it has met its aims. The objectives determine:

- how you structure and manage the outsourcing programme;
- which global delivery model you adopt;
- how you measure performance;
- what type of relationship your organization wants with the service provider.

Does your company want a long-term relationship or are you aiming to send a simple development project overseas? As your organization's experience of offshoring develops it is likely that more complex projects will be outsourced. Application management becomes a significant issue: ongoing maintenance costs can be several times the cost of the initial development stage.

Although a decision may have been made to pursue offshore outsourcing, this does not mean that every department will share the same objectives and concerns at the outset. You need to interview key sponsors and stakeholders to understand their different perspectives. Identify individuals who have sufficient authority, influence or ability to make a significant contribution or a damaging intervention if their views are not properly taken into account. Aim to understand each stakeholder's perspective through open discussion and encourage contributions at relevant points during the offshore project. Senior management commitment and support will be needed throughout, so it makes sense to identify key milestones and plan to involve senior executives in decision-making at these stages. Once you have identified and understood the different stakeholder viewpoints you can begin to create a shared agenda for offshore outsourcing.

Business case analysis

The business case sets out the reasons, advantages and justification for the offshore project. It should demonstrate that offshore outsourcing is achievable, affordable and represents good value for money. It is also a valuable planning tool that supports informed decisions. As the project progresses, you will be able to complete sections covering costs and timescales more accurately and precisely. At the outset you may have little more than a base case detailing costs of the project if carried out in-house, but by the time a preferred supplier is selected there should be a full business case with validated assumptions. The business case should cover both financial and non-financial issues, including:

- **Strategic case:** Setting the project in a strategic context, describing the objectives and explaining the different stakeholder viewpoints.
- **Current services or base case:** Detailing the costs that would be incurred if the project were to be completed purely in-house. The emphasis needs to be on gathering comprehensive costing information, including hidden costs such as desktops and peripherals included in business unit budgets, training treated as a personnel cost and data centre costs buried in facilities management budgets. The aim here is to quantify the project costs and outputs in a meaningful way so that an accurate comparison can be made with the offshore solution.
- **Options analysis:** Assessing the different business models that could be adopted using onshore, near-shore and far-shore operations.
- **Benefits analysis:** Reviewing the non-financial benefits such as quality standards, access to additional resources and freeing up the in-house team to focus on core business objectives.
- **Cost analysis:** Pivotal to the decision to proceed with offshore outsourcing. It is important, but not always easy, to look beyond the short-term transition costs and focus on the whole project life costs. All cost data should be displayed in spreadsheets together with a detailed breakdown of assumptions used.
- **Sensitivity analysis:** Considering the impact on the business case of variations in the assumptions that lie behind the cost and benefit analyses. The process is applied to all variables to illustrate the best and worst case scenarios.

- **Risk analysis:** Indicating potential risks and countermeasures. Each risk should be scored against the likelihood of its occurrence and the severity of its impact.

Risk management

The geographical distance between your organization and the offshore team, language and cultural differences all add to the risks involved in offshore outsourcing. Risks need to be understood and managed to prevent or minimize damage to the project. The information required to describe, classify and effectively manage these risks is substantial and potentially complex, but needs to be thorough to avoid problems at a later stage. Use a structured risk management process, including the following steps:

1. **Risk identification:** Identify all potential risks and invite others in your organization to contribute so that you devise a comprehensive list.
2. **Potential causes:** Consider the underlying causes of the risks, documenting the circumstances that could trigger damage to the offshore project.
3. **Risk assessment:** Each risk should be evaluated against two criteria to determine its importance or significance:
   - the likelihood of the risk occurring, rated high, medium or low (alternatively on a scale of 1 to 10);
   - the impact of this event on the offshore project, also rated high, medium or low (or on a scale of 1 to 10).
4. **Countermeasures:** Devise actions to be taken to manage the causes and consequences of each potential risk. What can be achieved depends on the nature of the risk and the extent to which your organization or the service provider can control the underlying causes. Potential countermeasures include:
   - measures that stop the risk or problem from occurring or prevent any impact on the offshore project;
   - actions that limit the impact of the risk or reduce the likelihood of it posing a threat to the programme;
   - contingency plans, which describe actions to be taken should the risk materialize;
   - penalty clauses or insurance policies, which in effect pass the risk to the supplier or to a third-party.
5. **Risk management responsibilities:** Each risk should have an owner whose role is to plan, resource and monitor the countermeasures.

> **DEVELOPING BEST PRACTICES IN THE FINANCIAL SERVICES INDUSTRY**
>
> In America, some of the largest financial services companies are getting together to develop best practices for outsourcing live operations offshore. This sector has been at the forefront of the expanding offshore market in the USA. Application development and maintenance of legacy systems have been moved offshore for a number of years, but attention is now turning to the potential for offshore technical support for IT systems and infrastructure. Technical support staff and systems administrators based offshore work on real-time IT applications remotely over a network connection to the operational system. Server capacity management, network and firewall administration are all functions that could be handled offshore. The risks to be addressed include concerns about offshore access to live data and business critical systems, security management and the protection of intellectual property.
>
> Members of the New York-based Financial Services Technology Consortium (FSTC) – including J. P. Morgan Chase & Co., Bank of America, Citigroup and Wells Fargo & Co. – met in August 2003 to discuss how they could reduce offshore risks. Work is now underway to examine offshore security, privacy, business continuity and contract cancellation issues linked to offshore management of onshore applications. The FSTC is looking at how to protect confidential data like trade secrets and customer information and prevent them being disclosed or stolen by competitors, the outsourcing supplier or its employees.
>
> www.computerworld.com, www.fstc.org

STATEMENT OF REQUIREMENTS

Offshore outsourcing requirements have to be expressed with clarity and in detail. The goal is to produce specific and comprehensive written documents that specify the work to be done, so that a geographically distant, non-native English speaking team can fully understand your requirements. There are two key documents: the statement of requirements (or statement of work) and the service level agreement (see 'Service level agreement' on page 79).

The statement of requirements describes all the functions that the service provider is expected to undertake and the roles and responsibilities of both supplier and client. It must clearly define the scope of the work to be outsourced and interfaces with other IT activities. Other topics to be covered include:

- project plans including deliverables and milestones;
- target service levels;
- design constraints such as technical standards and system interface requirements;
- training and education requirements;

- user support requirements;
- performance measurement information and report requirements;
- security requirements;
- change control process;
- a definition of the supplier's responsibilities;
- a definition of the client's responsibilities;
- proposed charging structures;
- transition arrangements, including knowledge transfer.

These requirements should form the basis for all decisions in the selection of a service provider and the construction of the contract. Nothing should be left up in the air.

INVESTIGATING THE IT SERVICES MARKET

The global services market makes this task much more demanding. The strengths and weaknesses of individual countries are a primary concern and you should identify the country (or countries) that best meets your requirements first, then the service provider. Each country presents unique benefits and disadvantages that suppliers can do little to influence:

- IT salaries are influenced by various factors, but within each country there is only limited variation in the wage costs incurred by different suppliers.
- Social and geopolitical concerns can override the advantages offered by specific suppliers.
- Physical and time zone distances make it more difficult to manage and control the outsourcing relationship.
- The business environment can attract or deter offshore outsourcing business – local taxes, regulation, support for the offshore industry, ease of resolving legal disputes and the effectiveness of trade associations.
- The country's education system determines the standard and number of qualified IT professionals available within the country.
- Countries that offer potential new markets may be attractive to multinational companies setting up offshore subsidiaries.
- Language and cultural inheritance influences the ease with which UK companies can do business in different countries.

Chapter 5 provides general facts and figures for 18 of the leading offshore destinations, an overview of each country, the local offshore IT services industry and links to sources of further information.

Before your procurement begins in earnest there is a lot to be gained from talking to, and visiting, service providers in different countries. Make the most of this opportunity before you enter the more formal selection process. You can find out more about the services offered and learn from the suppliers' experiences on other projects. Use this intelligence to refine your statement of requirements and to ensure that the scope and objectives of your offshore project are sound.

These visits also help to promote your offshore project to the market. At this point you will be encouraging suppliers to bid for the contract. The best outsourcing companies have many possible business opportunities to pursue and you want them to invest time and effort in bidding for your offshore project. Submitting bids and negotiating deals can be an expensive and risky exercise. So explain to potential suppliers why your offshore project is an attractive business proposition. Your aim is to generate a number of competitive bids from well-qualified companies in the country (or countries) of your choice. You may also find it useful to issue an information pack to interested suppliers and a press release to local trade publications.

CHOOSING A SERVICE PROVIDER

To select the best supplier for your offshore project you need to define clearly and unambiguously what you want the service provider to do, devise the criteria used to evaluate the bids you receive, and be clear how you are going to manage your organization's relationships with the suppliers that compete for the work. You need to be sure that short-listed suppliers are both motivated and capable of providing the required services.

The selection process described below is best suited to a medium-sized to large organization seeking to outsource a project that would otherwise be carried out by the in-house IT department. It can be adapted as necessary for different circumstances. Some organizations have specialist purchasing units that take the lead on elements of this selection process. The whole process is described here so that you can see where tasks completed by the IT department fit into the bigger picture.

Evaluation

You need a formal evaluation process that is auditable, consistent and ensures that a level playing field is adopted across all potential suppliers. The evaluation method and criteria should be developed in parallel with the preparation of the business case and statement of requirements and should be agreed before you contact potential suppliers to help ensure an objective assessment. A formal evaluation panel may be set-up, including representatives from business areas, the finance department and other key stakeholders. You need to decide how much information is going to be given to potential suppliers about the evaluation process and whether they are going to be offered feedback on the outcome.

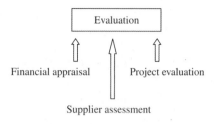

Figure 4.3 *Evaluation*

Relative wage rates are not the only important factor. The effectiveness of an offshore supplier also depends on the technical expertise available, the efficiency of their business processes and how well they relate to your organization. Even if wage rates are low, if projects take longer and need more resources the savings achieved in moving offshore may not be significant. Offshore suppliers' technical skills and business sector knowledge vary considerably.

As illustrated in Figure 4.3, the evaluation criteria typically include: supplier assessment, project evaluation and financial appraisal. Evaluation scores should be weighted to reflect business priorities.

Supplier assessment

You need to evaluate the service provider as a potential supplier to your organization.

- **Culture:** Does the service provider demonstrate the beliefs and values that your organization would look for in all its suppliers? How does the culture in the outsourcing company compare with your own organization? Will the two companies be able to work together comfortably?
- **Quality:** What is the supplier's approach to quality management? Has it achieved a recognized standard and has this been independently audited in the last two years? Does your own organization have the processes in place to work at the same quality standard as the supplier?
- **Responsiveness:** How quickly does the supplier respond to requests? How willing is it to adapt proposals to meet customer concerns? Does the supplier understand, and respond to, its customers' business priorities?
- **Maturity and experience:** How long has the supplier offered outsourced services? How many customers does it have? Is it financially stable? What are its future prospects? Is any of the work likely to be subcontracted? If so, where and to which company or companies? How well does the supplier work with other service providers?

- **Cultural awareness:** What education and training does the supplier give to its own staff to help them work effectively with UK organizations? Does the supplier have UK-based employees?
- **Process and methodologies:** Does the supplier use tried and tested processes for managing offshore projects? Is there evidence that these have worked successfully for other clients?

  For this aspect of the evaluation you need to investigate each potential supplier's track record and other clients' experiences. Ask for a full customer list and select three to five so that you have a better chance of getting a balanced assessment. Contact these customers yourself and explore their views on the supplier's performance.

Don't forget that the suppliers will also be evaluating your organization as a potential customer. They too will have questions about your company's culture, integrity and approach to quality management. They will want to determine whether this is a one-off offshore project or whether your organization might want to develop a more long-lasting relationship.

Project Evaluation

You will need to assess whether the supplier has the capability and technical ability to deliver your offshore project:

- the range of technical skills available within the service provider;
- the scale of resources available;
- integration experience and achievements working with other suppliers, including development of interfaces to other systems;
- specific industry experience, where relevant;
- proposed project team membership, level of experience and formal qualifications;
- transition and knowledge transfer plans;
- project management methodology.

Financial Appraisal

The evaluation should establish whether the supplier's proposals are financially sound and will deliver value for money, balancing costs and quality throughout the contract period. A key factor in offshore outsourcing is the number of full time equivalent (FTE) resources assigned to your project. The evaluation should look not only at the FTE numbers, but also at the different roles in the project team. This helps you to assess how well the supplier has understood the requirement and whether the team size and hence estimated project cost is reasonable and reliable.

You also need to determine the financial stability and future prospects of potential suppliers. There is a good deal of merger and acquisition activity in the offshore market and you should be alert to the possibility of any developments that might affect your service provider.

Short listing potential suppliers

The next step in the selection process is to draw up a short-list of service providers. Aim for a list of around three service providers (never less than two and ideally not more than five). Depending on the significance of your offshore project and the number of potential suppliers, a short list can be produced in two different ways:

- By reviewing marketing literature, annual reports and other written material about different suppliers' achievements and service offerings. Published case studies and conference presentations will give you feedback about other customers' experiences with various service providers.

- By requesting information from a number of potential suppliers and formally evaluating their responses (including a review of written material about the suppliers). This process is sometimes referred to as Request for Information (RFI) or inviting 'expressions of interest' from suppliers. The objective is to identify service providers who would all be capable of meeting your project requirements, offering value for money and developing effective outsourcing relationships. This approach is helpful with larger offshore projects and facilitates a more detailed analysis of the services your organization could source offshore. A short questionnaire should be sent to about 12 potential suppliers together with a project outline. Questions should cover topics such as skills base, charges, technical expertise, resource availability, company accounts, number of employees and client base.

Selecting the preferred bidder

This stage is launched by the issue of a Request for Proposals (RFP) to the short list of suppliers. A package of information is distributed including:

- Background information about your organization, its business strategy and goals, the project to be outsourced and any relevant corporate policies.

- A confidentiality statement, designed to protect the interests of both your organization and the suppliers during the selection process when commercially sensitive data may be exchanged.

- Description of the selection and evaluation process, with a planned timetable. The suppliers should be given clear, practical guidance about the submission of tender documents, the handling of pre-tender enquiries and so on.

- The statement of requirements describing all the functions that the service provider is expected to deliver and the roles and responsibilities of both the supplier and your organization.

- Guidance on the presentation of cost information and any constraints such as a maximum bid threshold above which it would be uneconomic for your organization to proceed with offshore outsourcing. Suppliers should be asked to present their costs in a specified format to help in the evaluation of bids and comparisons between the different service providers. Preferred charging formulae should be described where appropriate.

- A draft contract produced by your organization to ensure that it is in the driving seat and to make comparisons of the bids easier. This gives your organization the first advantage at the outset of negotiations and guides suppliers to the key features of your requirements. Potential contractual difficulties are thus raised at an early stage for resolution. Experienced suppliers may put forward their own draft contract, but this is unlikely to be helpful and forces your organization to argue for changes, giving the supplier the advantage.

- Transition and contract management plans, including the management structure you plan to put in place to oversee the offshore project. Suppliers should be asked to provide information on how they will manage and successfully complete the knowledge transfer process, and the numbers of staff involved.

To rely simply on written communication with potential suppliers would be unwise. Bidders need to be able to interact with your organization to fully understand your objectives and requirements. This should be arranged in such a way that you can maintain the level playing field between suppliers. You may arrange briefings to which all bidders are invited or offer the opportunity for site visits to your organization. Suppliers are likely to have many detailed queries as they prepare their bids, so make arrangements for questions to be answered promptly and accurately. Remember that any additional information given to one bidder must be shared with all suppliers to ensure a fair competition.

The responses received from the short-listed suppliers may be lengthy and evaluating the bids will require a considerable effort. The evaluation framework and criteria defined before the selection process began now directs how your organization selects the preferred bidder. The assessment of each supplier should take into account their written proposal and feedback on intelligence gathered during site visits and other discussions. The evaluation should be systematic, objective and well documented and seen to be so. The aim of this evaluation stage is to select the service provider that is most likely to deliver your project to time and budget, to offer best value for money and to be reliable, open and trustworthy.

Due diligence

Due diligence is especially important in offshore deals when your organization will be dependent on a distant workforce and an overseas organization that will probably be very unfamiliar and untried. It is an in-depth assessment and confirmation of details on which the contract will be based. Due diligence generally takes place after the main contract clauses are agreed but before the contract is signed. Although we will look in this section at the checks your organization, as the prospective client, will carry out, the supplier will also benefit from the due diligence process and may want to delve further into the assumptions that underpin your offshore project, identifying risks and checking the accuracy of the financial statements your organization has provided.

In the due diligence process you are confirming the service provider's claims about their company, their capabilities and level of relevant expertise. You are checking that they can deliver your project at the price and quality offered and that the infrastructure required will be in place and functioning reliably when it is needed. Due diligence can reveal significant issues that require further work and may affect contract prices. There are five areas that can be covered in the due diligence process, described below.

Price

Significant savings can be made using offshore outsourcing but you need to make sure that the prices quoted are realistic and reliable. You must check that the supplier has fully understood the project requirements; accurately estimated the number of staff required, the level of seniority and the technical skills needed; and taken into account any necessary expenditure on infrastructure, license fees and so on.

Solution

Does the team proposed have the necessary programming language and application skills and experience? You need to check their qualifications and previous project experience. Examine the processes, tools and methodology to be used on your project – there is often considerable variation within outsourcing companies, even those accredited at CMM Level 5. What counts is what will be used on your project. Map out the relevant processes and reconcile the differences between the supplier's procedures and your organization's before beginning your offshore project. Check the project plans in detail to assure yourself that the project can be delivered on time and within budget. Are change management and testing processes well organized and fully documented? You need to confirm security arrangements, disaster recovery and contingency plans.

Company

Examine the supplier's corporate structure, ownership, financial statements, future prospects, total number of employees and staff retention rates. Review the senior management team, customer base and subcontractor relationships.

Customer references

Follow up references in organizations similar to your own, where the nature of the offshore project is also comparable. A confident supplier will be happy for you to choose your reference sites – be wary if the service provider urges you to visit only specific customers. Use these contacts to check perceptions of the supplier's performance as well as results delivered. This is an opportunity to learn how to get the best from the supplier as well as reassuring your organization about past performance. Review the other customers' reasons for selecting the supplier, implementation experiences, technical integration and management performance, management of subcontractors, contractual compliance, problem resolution and overall satisfaction with the supplier.

Contractual

Any guarantees, subcontractor agreements, warranties and so on to be included in the contract need to be checked out. The supplier will probably want to carry out due diligence on your organization too, examining documents such as software license agreements and insurance policies.

> **BRITANNIA AIRWAYS**
>
> As reported in *Computing*, Britannia signed a £7 million offshore applications management and IT support deal with LogicaCMG in February 2004. The five-year contract covers the management, support and enhancement of more than 120 of the airline's IT applications. 'A prerequisite to achieving the optimum balance of outsourcing includes a careful analysis of strategy, business requirements, resources, the future market and a review of existing IT and business systems,' said Neil Boulton, head of IT at Britannia Airways. 'The move becomes more complicated, however, when you look at an environment in which you have no experience. You'll probably sign deals with companies that you've never dealt with before, and they might not have the reference material you're looking for.' To overcome these concerns, Britannia chose LogicaCMG, a supplier with whom it had an existing five-year relationship. This gave Britannia extra confidence and assurance that delivery dates would be met. A hybrid outsourcing model was adopted, combining onshore and offshore working. The management of the services is based at Luton, while the Bangalore development centre handles the design, development and implementation of software

> solutions and products, and application management services. This means that 20 per cent of the work stays in the UK and Britannia works with Luton rather than Bangalore on a day-to-day basis.
>
> 'We run a 24 hour, seven days-a-week operation and going offshore has made this more cost effective,' said Neil Boulton. 'If we spot a problem late afternoon in the UK, LogicaCMG in India can work on it and resolve it overnight, before the next working day. Although we've always worked on this 24 hour basis, we now have a more cost-effective delivery.'
>
> www.computing.co.uk

OUTSOURCING CONTRACTS

We have seen that offshore outsourcing carries a number of potential risks. Control and risk mitigation are therefore key concerns and the outsourcing contract plays an important role in protecting the interests of your organization. Don't be tempted to forge ahead without a sound contract – if you do run into problems there will be no backstop to protect your organization from serious damage. Your legal department or other legal advisors will clearly play a major role in the construction of the outsourcing contract. What follows is an outline of the major topics to be covered.

The aim should be to agree a fair and comprehensive contract. The deal should be carefully balanced with neither side significantly disadvantaged. It should be expressed in clear and precise terms. Legal terminology should be avoided where possible, since it can often be confusing. This is particularly important if your supplier's first language is not English. Both supplier and customer must be able to understand the contract without difficulty. You do not want to waste time while people try to work out what the contract means.

The process of preparing, discussing and seeking agreement about the outsourcing contract is itself very beneficial as it forces both your organization and the supplier to address all issues and concerns before a commitment is made to the offshore project. Difficult and sensitive topics have to be tackled rather than avoided. The outsourcing relationship can then begin on a sound footing, with both parties having a deep understanding of the agreement.

Contract structure

There is no standard outsourcing contract and each offshore project has its own unique set of requirements. The contract can be structured in different ways and what follows describes one model framework. The contract will consist of main clauses covering general terms and conditions together with service particulars, and a series of schedules including the service level agreement and price details. The contract main clauses include:

- **General provisions:** For example, definitions and governing law.
- **Contract duration:** Possibly with provision for extension periods.
- **Change control:** A contract clause specifying that both parties will comply with the principles and processes detailed in a contract schedule.
- **Audit rights:** These give your organization the right to examine the supplier's records to confirm that you are receiving the quality of service agreed and are being billed accurately for the services delivered.
- **Confidentiality and data protection:** This ensures that any personal or commercially sensitive information is protected. The contract should require both parties to keep each other's information confidential and ensure that employees, contractors and advisors do likewise. If personal data will be processed in the project, you need to be confident that the contract contains sufficient measures to ensure compliance with the Data Protection Act.
- **Intellectual property:** All assets that form part of the outsourcing deal, including telecommunications equipment, third-party contracts and software licenses should be listed, with details included in schedules.
  - **Software developed by your organization:** A license should be granted formally to the supplier to use any software created by your organization and used in the offshore project. The contract should make it clear whether your organization will retain the intellectual property rights in the software once the supplier starts to modify the application.
  - **Software developed by the supplier:** The contract should make provision for the intellectual property rights associated with software written for the offshore project to be assigned to your organization.
  - **Software developed by third parties:** You need to be sure that any software created by a third party and transferred to your supplier to use in the offshore project is correctly licensed for use and that ownership is clearly defined. The major offshore suppliers may have their own licensing arrangements in place for commonly used applications. In all other circumstances you need to start negotiations with third-party software providers as soon as practical. The analysis of rights and restrictions in existing third-party software licenses is often a major exercise.
- **Security provisions:** An overview of the policies and standards to be adopted are included in the main contract, with detailed procedures and practices described in a schedule.

- **Service particulars:** Based on the statement of requirements (see 'Statement of requirements' on page 67) and outlining project deliverables and milestones, optional service extensions, framework for transition and knowledge transfer, quality policies, performance measures and reports, contract management structure and meetings.

- **Charges and charging structure:** Precise charging formulae, tax issues, detailed invoicing and payment procedures are included as a schedule and general principles in the main contract. You need to agree how fluctuations in currency will affect charges and who bears the currency risk.

- **Managing poor performance:** The aim is to address minor faults without delay and encourage good performance. Careful consideration needs to be given before financial remedies are specified. If excessive, the supplier may become overly defensive and increase prices. Measures to discourage poor performance may include cash refunds and service credits. Agreed escalation procedures should be included in a schedule so that faults can be remedied as quickly and as efficiently as possible. A *force majeure* clause will cover instances where failure to meet contractual commitments is beyond the reasonable control of either party.

- **Warranties, liabilities and indemnities:** Warranties are representations made by the service provider, for example relating to performance, breach of which entitles the client to claim damages. Indemnities provide for compensation payable for specific losses, for example for breach of data protection requirements. Limits to the provider's liability for default or under an indemnity need to be carefully negotiated and should be both reasonable and realistic.

- **Dispute resolution principles:** The first objective is to manage the outsourcing contract in such a way as to minimize the likelihood of disputes arising. But the contract should include structured dispute resolution procedures, defining responsibilities and steps that will be taken before legal proceedings are initiated. The main contract should include a statement of the principles with detailed procedures defined in a contract schedule.

- **Contract termination:** Setting down the procedures and rules that will apply. If the agreement has run its full term, the contract will need to specify everything needed to ensure a smooth handover either back to your organization or to another supplier. Where the contract is terminated early, notice periods and compensation arrangements need to be defined.

> **DATA PROTECTION ISSUES**
>
> A group of UK Labour MEPs, representing the trade union Amicus, called on the European Commission in 2004 to extend data protection laws to cover customer information handled overseas. The MEPs also wanted companies to be forced to allow overseas call centre staff to disclose their real names and their location to customers. Problems experienced by US credit card company Capital One and insurance company Axa raised concerns about the impact of offshoring. Capital One pulled out of India after call centre operators offered unauthorized credit levels to customers. The Evening Standard newspaper reported that organized gangs had offered the equivalent of a year's salary to call-centre staff in return for access to UK credit card details. Axa relocated some Indian customer service jobs to its head office in Leicester after problems with the processing of applications for small and medium-sized firms. David Fleming, national secretary for finance at Amicus said, 'Offshoring is an accident waiting to happen. It is only a matter of time before a serious crime is committed which will ruin the reputation of the British financial services industry.'
>
> The Information Commissioner's Office, which enforces the Data Protection Act, was not so concerned. 'We have never taken any action against firms that have broken the Data Protection Act by offshoring,' said a spokeswoman. 'One of the principles of the Act is that companies should not outsource to countries that are not in the EU unless strict contracts are in place, but we are talking about big firms that are aware of the issues.'
>
> www.computerweekly.com, www.silicon.com, news.bbc.co.uk

Service level agreement

The service level agreement is one of the most important components of the outsourcing contract. The agreement defines the level of performance that the supplier has contracted to provide and gives the client rights and remedies should the supplier fail to deliver this level of service. It can act as an effective incentive to encourage your supplier to meet your objectives for the outsourced project. Although the service level agreement is usually a schedule to the main contract, it should be written in terms that everyone working on the project can readily understand rather than in legal language. Try to avoid a multiplicity of interrelated performance measures and service levels that only a few people fully understand. Keep things simple and focus on the core requirements.

The service level agreement is very much a living document that is in regular use in the management of the outsourcing relationship. Once formally agreed, its contents should be widely disseminated among onshore and offshore team members. Everyone should be clear about what is expected of them, so that they can work towards project targets and be aware of any penalties that will apply if the standards are not met.

Service level agreements need to be kept up-to-date. They should regularly be reviewed to ensure that they continue to meet business needs and the outsourcing objectives. Changes may be requested at any time and should be handled through the normal change control process. The main topics covered by the service level agreement are listed below:

- Introduction:
    - project name and brief description;
    - scope of agreement;
    - names of parties to the agreement;
    - start and end dates.
- Description of project:
    - outline of project plans;
    - link to business and IT strategies;
    - deliverables;
    - milestones;
    - roles and responsibilities of users, in-house IT team and supplier team (onshore and offshore).
- Quality management:
    - quality standards to be applied to project;
    - compliance with international standards such as ISO 9000;
    - audit arrangements.
- Security and data protection:
    - policies and practices to be adopted;
    - compliance with international standards such as ISO 15408;
    - audit arrangements;
    - disaster recovery and contingency plans.
- Outputs:
    - project products;
    - project progress and performance reports;
    - management information reports.
- Charging:
    - invoicing procedures and targets;
    - payment terms (actual charges may be listed in a separate contract schedule for ease of use and confidentiality reasons).
- Refunds and service credits:
    - criteria that trigger refunds and credits;
    - procedures for making refunds and credits.
- Interfaces:
    - specifications of the links between this project and other initiatives and operational systems;
    - procedures for resolving disputes between different suppliers over causes of project failures.

- Performance review:
  - frequency and type of project progress review meetings.

Negotiations

The aim of negotiations is to deal with all outstanding issues in a way that leaves each party content that they have struck a fair deal and that the relationship between them will enhance the business performance of both organizations. The following guidelines will help your company adopt a constructive approach:

- Use logical persuasion and explain your interests in a businesslike manner.
- Aim to decide issues on their merits rather than seek to impose your view.
- Focus on interests, not positions: be definite but flexible.
- Look for mutual gains wherever possible.
- Be creative: look for alternative solutions when your organization and the supplier cannot agree.
- Acknowledge the supplier's legitimate interests and the wider context from their point of view.

It is important that both parties start from a position of equal strength. The supplier will have been involved in many negotiations – make sure that your organization is not at a disadvantage and recruit an expert advisor if you do not have sufficient skills in-house. If your organization has identified one preferred bidder, choose a reserve bidder and make sure that both suppliers are aware of this. Alternatively some organizations choose to negotiate in parallel with two potential suppliers to maintain a strong competition for as long as possible.

Negotiations require careful and comprehensive planning. Several hours' preparation is needed for each hour spent in negotiation. The complexity of international outsourcing agreements requires a blend of business and legal expertise during negotiations. Anyone involved in negotiating an offshore project can expect to spend many hours travelling to and from the offshore destination.

Contract award

The final issues have been resolved; a little give and take by both parties has produced a contract that is duly signed. This is a significant milestone, but it is only a step along the way. Celebrate the contract award by all means, but remember:

- Don't put the contract in the bottom of a cupboard and forget about it – it is a vital risk management tool.

- Use the contract as a sound foundation and a guide to help you get the best from your offshore project.
- Don't pin the contract on the wall and refer to it every time you speak to the supplier – this is not the way to develop a constructive outsourcing relationship.
- All too often those involved in negotiating the deal move on, leaving no one who really understands what was agreed. Make sure that there is continuity and knowledge about the contract in the team overseeing the project.

TRANSITION

The implementation of the outsourcing contract or transition from in-house to offshore project should be well managed just as any other IT programme. In a traditional onshore deal, staff often transfer with the project or IT function to the supplier, taking with them an understanding of applications, infrastructure and associated business processes. Offshore outsourcing is quite different and an entire project or function may be handed over to a new team. Knowledge transfer is therefore a key element in any offshore transition plan. You need to free up sufficient in-house staff time to educate and train the offshore team – not in the core technical skills, but in the specific applications used in your organization, the interfaces to be built in the offshore project, the users' perspective on the project and the way your organization works. This is a resource-intensive stage when IT operations must continue as before even though the knowledge transfer process takes up a lot of staff time.

The supplier will need to send experienced staff from the new offshore team to your organization as required during transition. These employees will become critical to the successful completion of the offshore project to time and budget. Staff retention can be a problem for the most skilled employees and you should seek assurances from your supplier that they will do all they can to keep the same key personnel on your offshore project from start to finish. At worst you will find yourself constantly arranging training for staff newly appointed to the offshore team.

Your organization should appoint its own project manager and not rely entirely on the supplier's manager. Plan for your in-house team to shift their working hours at this stage. If the offshore team has a problem or needs information they may want to talk to your organization. Before transition begins make sure that process flowcharts, system documentation and project management records are fully updated so that they are ready to be shared with the offshore team.

Although the supplier will lead the overall transition programme and will be responsible for many of the activities, your organization will also have a number of responsibilities, particularly tasks that involve internal communications. Transition activities include:

- detailed project planning;
- transfer of responsibility for the offshore project;
- set-up and introduction of governance structures;
- implementation of contract management process including invoicing and payment procedures;
- introduction of change request processes (there may be a backlog if project requirements were frozen during the selection of supplier and negotiations);
- implementation of problem management and escalation procedures;
- risk mitigation activities;
- communications programme;
- career development help and support for those staff whose work is moving overseas;
- liaison with trade unions or other employee representatives.

Don't be tempted to hand over responsibility for the project too early. Adjust your plans if the offshore team is not ready. If your organization is new to offshore outsourcing it pays to allow extra time for transition. Don't assume that every supplier is an expert in transition management.

MANAGING PERFORMANCE

To get the best from the offshore team, you need to tackle the challenges of managing a remote outsourced service. As with any outsourcing relationship you need to develop a good working relationship with your supplier, share your vision of what can be achieved, monitor financial issues closely and regularly review key performance indicators (KPIs). But there is an added dimension when the project team is overseas – the potential for cultural misunderstandings, the possible use of different terminology and the need to give detailed and precise instructions that you may not easily be able to discuss with a team working in a different time zone.

To manage the outsourcing relationship effectively and derive the anticipated benefits for your organization, a skilled in-house team is needed. Companies entering outsourcing deals all too often neglect this. As Gartner's Roger Cox has commented,

> **The big issues arise once the ink has dried on the contract, when the business is left with just a few people who understand the contract. Users need to build a deal around a governance structure to manage change.**
> **www.computerweekly.com.**

You need strong processes between your organization and the supplier.

Developing outsourcing relationships

Successful relationships don't just happen overnight – they need commitment, a cooperative approach and a constructive attitude. You will be working closely alongside a team based in a foreign land, from a different cultural background and historical context. It pays to take time to learn a little more about the country, its people, traditions and values. Based on my own experience and research I have developed a set of key principles for building outsourcing relationships as illustrated in Figure 4.4. The following guidelines will help you develop an effective relationship with your supplier:

- Work towards an open and honest relationship that is built on mutual trust. Explain to your supplier that you are looking for this type of relationship. You will naturally be looking for the supplier to demonstrate a track record of delivering on promises and contractual commitments. But remember that this is a two-way process and ensure that your organization is trustworthy and meets its commitments, for example to pay agreed invoices promptly.

- Recognize that both parties need to benefit from the relationship and the supplier is justified in seeking a reasonable profit margin. Look for win–win solutions.

- A cooperative approach will pay dividends. In the longer term, domination by either party will damage the relationship. This does not mean accepting every suggestion that the supplier makes and there will be areas of disagreement. But look for a constructive solution

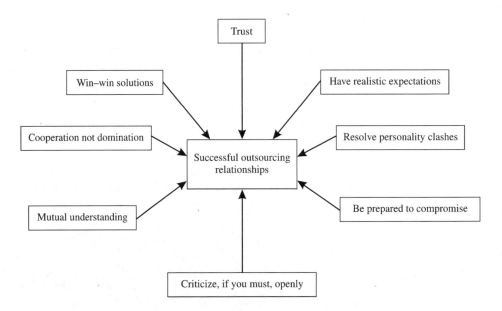

Figure 4.4 *Successful outsourcing relationships*

without trying to force the supplier into a tight corner – this will only lead to resentment.

- Good communication is critically important. Work towards an environment in which information is readily shared. Set-up links at all levels between your organization and the supplier. Share celebrations and recognize good service as well as expressing concern or complaining about failures.
- Introduce your stakeholders to the offshore team. Let the supplier know about the expectations and concerns expressed within your organization about offshoring. Share your company's plans, business objectives and organizational structure with your supplier. Take an active interest in the fortunes of your supplier. Theses steps will help foster mutual understanding between your two organizations.
- When you need to criticize poor performance do so openly and recognize that your supplier may have a different perspective.
- Be prepared to compromise without losing sight of your overall objectives.
- Resolve personality clashes before they get out of hand and damage more than just a relationship between two people.
- Expect success but do not encourage unrealistic expectations.

Communication

Outsourcing introduces a whole new set of roles and responsibilities into your organization. This can be confusing and create doubt and concern. Everyone involved needs to understand their role and how to get things done. The introduction of offshore working is often a period of turmoil and readjustment as people adapt to a new way of working.

Communication is a vital element in the successful introduction of offshore working and should absorb a major part of every manager's working day. You will already be aware of the need for effective communication between your team and the user community. This becomes more of a challenge when project team members work in another country and you need to maintain good communication between the supplier's project team both onshore and offshore, the in-house IT department and the user community.

When projects are carried out offshore, users rely on you more than usual for progress information. By openly reporting back on progress and difficulties, and by having contingency measures ready if problems occur, you can encourage the users to have a realistic picture of the project and to be confident that you have proper control over the outsourcing process.

One of the advantages of offshore outsourcing is that you can use the different time zones to extend the working day. You therefore often depend on email communication or telephone messages, since it won't always be possible to talk to the offshore team. You need to ensure that you have processes in place to deal promptly with messages and emails. Communications need to be clear and unambiguous, avoiding slang and jargon familiar only within your organization. Combine different forms of communication: telephone, email, videoconferencing and collaborative portals to suit different purposes. Communicate early and often and allow time for the outsourcing relationship to mature: don't expect liaison to work well from day one.

Invest time and money in visiting your offshore location. IT professionals from your organization will learn a great deal from short assignments working with the offshore team, experiencing the offshore team's work environment and the project from their perspective. Managers should visit the offshore team several times each year to further deepen and develop the relationship between your two organizations.

Special arrangements need to be made for anyone who will lose their role as a result of work moving offshore. They may feel angry, sad, resentful, worried or rebellious and this is only natural. In fact if these members of staff show no emotion you should be concerned because it may mean that they are not facing up to the reality of the offshore project. These individuals should receive key information from their own senior managers, in person as well as through general briefings, contact with the personnel department, personalized letters, dedicated enquiry points and newsletters.

Contract management and administration

The contract management team should be in place before the contract is signed so that your organization is in control and monitoring the project from the start. Make sure that you have suitably qualified people in the team and provide any necessary training. Contract management today is far more than administering contract changes and processing invoices. You need to invest rather more resources in contract management for offshore projects than for traditional onshore outsourcing.

Speaking at a BCS London (Central) Branch meeting in 2003, Ian Puddy, director of consulting at Gartner, stressed the importance of the team set-up to manage the outsourcing relationship and contract:

> Organizations sometimes think they can throw it over the wall to another organization – but they're sadly mistaken. Good contracts are not set in stone – a contract is not built to last until you fall out – they're built to change, to respond to the organization's changing needs. This is why having an internal team is absolutely paramount – you must manage the contract.

The responsibilities of the contract management function include:

- monitoring compliance with the contract, balancing the cost of monitoring against the risk of problems occurring;
- disseminating information about the contract and agreeing contract interpretations with the supplier;
- managing the contract change process;
- resolving minor disputes;
- monitoring the total value of the deal, business benefits delivered and expenditure;
- reviewing delivery against overall outsourcing objectives.

Your organization needs to introduce a number of administrative procedures and clerical functions to support the outsourcing contract. The procedures should be designed to reflect the scope and complexity of the outsourcing contract and your organization's policies and business processes, and include:

- contract maintenance;
- charges and cost monitoring;
- ordering procedures;
- payment procedures;
- budget management;
- performance reporting.

Service management and key performance indicators

When integrated and managed properly, offshore resources can both reduce operating costs and increase service levels. But to achieve these benefits you need to set-up a service management function to monitor service levels to assess whether agreed performance targets are met and maintain service quality and technology interface standards. From the start you need baseline measurements for existing performance levels against which future improvements (or deterioration) can be compared. You need to appoint a service control team, whose members have a good understanding of the project requirements and technical environment. The team's responsibilities will include:

- monitoring the transition and knowledge transfer phase;
- analysing service management standards through the supplier's adherence to best practices such as the Information Technology Infrastructure Library (ITIL) standards;
- monitoring the effectiveness of procedures such as contingency plans, back-up procedures and test procedures;
- resolving service issues and problems.

To measure the performance of your supplier you need to collect and review a series of measurements. At one extreme you might collect a lot of data, which is at best of limited value and at worst misleading if it focuses attention away from key areas. It is important to identify the critical factors and devise KPIs that enable your organization to assess how effectively the supplier is meeting your objectives. The KPIs should be designed to point the supplier's behaviour in the right direction. They should also reflect what is good service in the eyes of the project sponsor and stakeholders.

Look for advantages and benefits in your outsourcing deal beyond simple cost savings. You may get added value by encouraging your supplier to offer suggestions for improving or even transforming processes, systems and infrastructure. Aim for a culture of continuous improvement in the management of the offshore project.

Change control

As we have seen, offshore outsourcing works best where requirements are stable, but inevitably some changes will be needed during the life of the contract. A formal change control process ensures that your organization understands the value it will gain and the costs that will be incurred by modifying the requirements. You need a step-by-step process for proposing, costing, agreeing and implementing changes. A fast-track process should be designed to handle urgent requests.

Resolving problems

Every project raises some unexpected issues – aim to identify potential difficulties before they become significant problems. Don't rely on written progress reports alone. Question the offshore team about what they have achieved, get into the detail of areas that are raising concerns and use visits to the offshore location to confirm progress.

Introduce a well-defined escalation process that identifies the priority of each issue raised and allocates time limits for the resolution of problems. Make sure that you maintain order during the escalation process without either side going straight to the top and bypassing agreed procedures. Try to find a resolution that costs your organization little but gives your supplier a face saving way to agree with you.

If the outsourcing relationship deteriorates beyond an acceptable level, your organization may decide to adopt more formal methods of dispute resolution – arbitration or legal proceedings. Such a decision should not, however, be taken lightly. Legal action is costly and disruptive and there are no guarantees that your organization will benefit from the outcome. Far better to carefully select your supplier and negotiate a contract that safeguards against disputes arising that cannot readily be resolved.

5 Country Profiles

The global offshore market is dynamic and growing rapidly. It is also diversifying, offering a wide range of services from many different countries. We need to take a global perspective when we consider how best to source IT services and facilities, but the potential choice of suppliers is enormous. In traditional, onshore IT outsourcing the supplier's location is relatively unimportant and the focus is on selecting the best-qualified service provider. There is no particular advantage or disadvantage in choosing a supplier based in Southampton, Birmingham or Newcastle. The IT staff providing the services will work wherever they are needed. This is not so in offshore sourcing when the work is carried out offsite in another country. Each country offers distinct benefits and problems, which will have a powerful influence over any company offering IT services. The suppliers have little or no influence over some of these factors:

- **Labour costs** depend on local economic conditions, government policies and exchange rates.
- **Socio and geopolitical factors** affect a country's stability and may disrupt normal business operations.
- **Physical distance and time zone differences** affect how easily people can get together for meetings and videoconferences or to speak by telephone.
- **The business environment** is created by each country's approach to regulation, tax, intellectual property protection and so on.
- **Market prospects** make some countries particularly attractive to companies looking to expand.

Offshore service providers have some influence over other factors:

- **Communications** depend on a shared language and UK companies look for good spoken and written English skills. We are fortunate in that English is so widely spoken around the world, but good communications also need a shared technical language, an understanding of accents, colloquialisms and even body language. The best offshore companies recruit staff with excellent English skills and in addition provide communication training.
- **Culture** influences the way we work, the values we adopt and our deep-seated beliefs about the world around us. Each country has its own culture, but an offshore supplier can provide training so that their

staff understand British culture and can work more effectively with UK companies.
- **Infrastructure** can be unreliable or even unavailable in some offshore destinations. High-speed digital communications and a clean supply of continuous electrical power are needed. Inadequate infrastructure can be at least partly overcome by installing generators and private communications networks in specially created technology or business parks.
- **Availability of specialist skills** can be a problem, but offshore suppliers can work alongside universities and training providers to develop the competences needed in the IT services industry.

The first decision to make, therefore, is the choice of offshore destination. There are nine factors that need to be taken into account in reviewing countries as possible locations for offshore work:

- language skills – spoken and written English;
- cultural compatibility;
- government support – for the IT services industry and business in general;
- labour pool – size and skills base;
- educational system;
- infrastructure – telecommunications and power supply;
- data and intellectual property protection;
- political stability;
- cost.

Countries planning to develop their offshore IT services industry need a reliable electricity supply, good telecommunications links, a stable government and suitably qualified labour resources with a strong work ethic. The industry often develops near one or more universities or colleges and once a particular city or country gets a critical mass of outsourcing companies, other firms are naturally drawn to the same location.

The choice of country is particularly important to organizations looking to outsource projects directly to companies based overseas and to IT companies and large organizations wanting to set up local offices or build facilities in offshore locations. Others may choose to use services from companies based in Western Europe or the USA who themselves send work offshore to various countries. In all cases, dispersing work across several destinations can mitigate risks linked to any one country.

Remember that the market is going through a period of growth and consolidation, with company mergers and acquisitions commonplace. You need to keep a close watch on developments and monitor your supplier's financial results. Avoid being caught by surprise if your supplier runs into financial difficulties or even goes bankrupt. Always have a contingency plan ready should the worst happen. New suppliers in emerging markets may offer particularly tempting deals, but you should be wary of accepting a contract based on anything other than a sustainable value proposition. Unless your offshore project is non-critical and small scale be wary of being the first client of any new supplier.

Fundamental changes in Eastern Europe offer the potential to develop a thriving offshore IT services industry in the region. With the demise of communism, professionals previously employed by the military and other government bodies have looked for alternative jobs in IT organizations. Nearly all the software companies in this region are based in the major cities such as Budapest, Bucharest, Prague and Warsaw. These areas offer a relatively well-established telecommunications infrastructure, are located near a major university or government centre and provide ready access to sources of funding. Despite recent investments in communications infrastructure, the region still has a long way to go to reach the standards of service common throughout Western Europe. Excessive red tape and unhelpful laws still cause problems in some countries. But this is a region to watch. Much may change over the next few years, particularly in those countries that joined the EU in 2004 and are investing in modernizing their systems to comply with EU requirements. Countries like the Czech Republic, Poland and Hungary are increasingly attractive as near-shore destinations for European countries. Eventually EU membership may lead to a narrowing of wage differentials with the rest of Europe – the offshore advantage does not stand still and the quest for competitively priced quality IT services will continue.

Uganda, Togo, Senegal, Ghana and South Africa are among the African countries developing an offshore services industry. Senegal is the most popular destination in the French-speaking world, while Ghana and South Africa lead in the English-speaking markets. Africa represents a very small proportion of the global IT services industry, but even a tiny share of a multibillion dollar sector can be worth a lot to a developing economy.

US-based companies who are looking for relatively low geopolitical risk or need Spanish speakers favour Latin American countries. The call centre business is growing in countries such as Costa Rica, Argentina and the Caribbean Islands.

GENERAL INFORMATION RESOURCES

Any organization contemplating offshore sourcing needs to research potential locations. The following websites provide useful background data on all countries.

The Bag Lady

This online directory and international trading portal is aimed at women in business. It incorporates free access to country profiles based on United

Nations' data. The profiles are built to your requirements and can contain information on demographics, trade, legislation, business and social factors.

Visit www.the-bag-lady.co.uk for more information.

The Business Start Page

This Houston, Texas-based website offers advice and information on running and operating a business. Of particular interest is a page giving detailed information on international business address formats and personal salutations (www.bspage.com/address.html).

Visit www.bspage.com for more general information.

Country Watch

Country Watch provides information for private and public sector organizations, schools, universities, libraries and individuals who need up-to-date information and news on the countries of the world. Key political, economic and business information together with daily news is provided for each country.

Visit www.countrywatch.com for more information.

Economist Intelligence Unit

The Economist Intelligence Unit (EIU) is the business information arm of The Economist Group and a leading information provider for companies setting up and managing operations across national borders anywhere in the world. Established more than 50 years ago in London, the EIU has a worldwide network of offices including London, New York, Hong Kong, Vienna, Singapore and Tokyo. The EIU produces objective and timely analyses and forecasts of the political, economic and business environment in more than 180 countries.

EIU Viewswire (www.viewswire.com) provides detailed market information and analysis for each country. The ebusiness forum (www.ebusinessforum.com) offers information and analysis on the global digital economy including insights from the top experts, research, case studies, news briefings and prospects for ebusiness growth in 60 countries.

Executive Planet™

This website provides tips on business etiquette, customs and protocol for doing business worldwide. The Executive Planet™ Guides covering 42 countries are co-authored by experts in international business etiquette, who also answer questions submitted on the discussion board.

Visit www.executiveplanet.com for more information.

Hieros Gamos Employment Law

Created by an American company, this website provides access not only to USA employment information, but also to supranational organizations and other country's information sources.

Visit www.hg.org/employ.html for more information.

Information Technology Landscape in Nations Around the World

This website contains a collection of reports prepared by students at the Kogod School of Business, American University, Washington. The reports describe information technology and telecommunications in more than 80 countries. The white paper on offshore outsourcing is particularly useful.

Visit www.american.edu/academic.depts/ksb/mogit/country.html for more information.

International Growth

This website is provided by the DTI in partnership with UK Trade & Investment (a government organization) and Intellect. It offers a 'one-stop-shop' on the web for the UK software and computer services industry. The aim is to help UK companies exploit opportunities to grow their business through international trade by providing advice and information as well as linking to resources available through the internet. Of particular interest to companies contemplating offshore working are:

- **Country Research:** Regularly updated research reports covering major overseas markets including Brazil, Canada, India, Mexico, Russia, Singapore and South Africa. Each report covers the software and computer services sector, its history and future growth prospects and provides guidance on doing business in the country. The reports are produced under the auspices of the British embassies within each country and are available only to UK companies.
- **Web Resources:** Links to some of the best international business websites, offering help and advice on a wide range of subjects including:
    - market resources covering political, economic, legal, cultural and technological factors;
    - legal information and guidance on laws governing trade in various countries, including intellectual property rights and local employment legislation;
    - culture and business etiquette advice to help you develop the skills needed to manage people and conduct negotiations in different business environments.

Visit www.internationalgrowth.org for more information.

International Monetary Fund

The International Monetary Fund (IMF) is an international organization of 184 member countries. It was established to provide international monetary cooperation, exchange stability and orderly exchange arrangements; to foster economic growth and high levels of employment; and to provide temporary financial assistance to countries to help ease balance of payments adjustment. The site offers access to financial information, reports and papers on each country.

For more information visit www.imf.org.

Lonely Planet

Travel guides are a useful source of information about history, geography, politics and customs. They also provide important practical advice on climate, internal travel arrangements and national and local holidays. Lonely Planet is one of the best and its country guides include key facts and figures and sections on history and culture.

For more information visit www.lonelyplanet.com/destinations.

Organisation for Economic Co-operation and Development

The 30 member countries within the Organization for Economic Cooperation and Development (OECD) share a commitment to democratic government and the market economy. OECD's work covers economic and social issues from macroeconomics to trade, education, development, science and innovation. The website provides access to a range of education statistics for member countries.

Visit www.oecd.org for more information.

Techlocate

Techlocate is an inward investment consultancy that brings together companies looking to expand in Europe, the locations that are looking to attract them and the intermediaries that help the corporate expansion process. The consultancy's website provides general information, contact details for investment promotion agencies and related news for many European countries and major cities.

Visit www.techlocate.com for more information.

The World Bank Group: Data and Statistics

Drawing on data produced by the official statistical systems organized and financed by national governments, the World Bank compiles a range of reports and comparative analyses. The World Development Indicators database provides information on population, life expectancy, primary education and malnutrition. Country data is available for ICT (information and communication technologies) infrastructure and access, computer and internet use, ICT expenditure, business and government environment. Other databases cover education, gender, health, nutrition and population statistics.

Visit www.worldbank.org/data for more information.

The World Information Technology and Services Alliance

The World Information Technology and Services Alliance (WITSA) is a consortium of over 50 IT industry associations from economies around the world. Its members represent over 90 per cent of the world IT market. As the global voice of the IT industry, WITSA aims to advocate policies that advance the sector's growth and development; and facilitate international trade and investment in IT products and services. Founded in 1978, WITSA is based in Virginia, USA and has become increasingly involved in international public policy issues such as:

- increasing competition through open markets and regulatory reform;
- protecting intellectual property;
- encouraging cross-industry and government cooperation to enhance information security;
- bridging the education and skills gap;
- reducing tariff and non-tariff barriers to trade in IT goods and services;
- safeguarding the viability and continued growth of the internet and electronic commerce.

The website offers IT industry information, white papers and links to WITSA member websites.

Visit www.witsa.org for more information.

World Intellectual Property Organization

The World Intellectual Property Organization (WIPO) is an international organization dedicated to promoting the use and protection of works of the human spirit – intellectual property. Based in Geneva, the WIPO is a United Nations agency and administers 23 international treaties dealing with different aspects of intellectual property protection.

Visit www.wipo.int for more information.

The WIPO Guide to Intellectual Property Worldwide (www.wipo.int/about-ip/en/ipworldwide) includes individual country profiles for each WIPO member state. The profiles cover legislation on patents, trademarks and industrial designs; copyright and related rights; membership of international treaties; and sources of further information.

Other useful web-based resources

- neoIT (2003) Research summary: Mapping offshore markets (www.neoit.com);
- Sourcing Interest Group (2003) Offshore outsourcing part one: State of the industry (www.sourcinginterests.org);
- Computerworld (2003) Knowledge center: Offshore buyer's guide (www.computerworld.com/managementtopics/outsourcing);
- OutsourcingCenter, an internal portal offering access to free research, case studies, market intelligence and online outsourcing journals (www.outsourcing-center.com).

KEY TO COUNTRY PROFILES

The following sections provide an introduction to many of the offshore destinations active in today's global IT services industry. The profiles are divided into five subsections:

- A brief introduction to the country, based on information from the Lonely Planet website and the EIU Viewswire service.
- Key facts and figures extracted from the Bag Lady Country profiles, EIU Viewswire and the World Bank data resources. The EIU country risk scores and business environment indices were recorded in August 2004. The World Bank's ICT business and government environment ratings are taken from the World Economic Forum's Global Competitiveness Report 2002–03 and Global Information Technology Report 2002–03. The ratings are based on opinion surveys of more than 4,700 senior business leaders from 80 countries.
- An overview of the offshore IT services industry.
- A brief description of one or more of the leading local IT services companies or multinational companies based in the country.
- Useful information sources specific to the country, including trade associations.

Health warning

The sections that follow provide statistics about the offshore market in different countries, the numbers of qualified IT professionals and average salaries. During the course of my research for this book I have visited many different websites of varying quality and read articles from a number of different magazines and newspapers. Statistics quoted in these sources are not always consistent and it is not always possible to confirm the accuracy of the data. This is compounded by variations caused by fluctuations in exchange rates. I have avoided unreliable sources, statistics that are out-of-date and websites that do not appear to be actively maintained. Nevertheless it is advisable to treat these offshore industry statistics with a degree of caution.

UNITED KINGDOM

To help you put the country data into context, equivalent figures and ratings for the UK are given below.

FACTS AND FIGURES

Full country name	United Kingdom of Great Britain and Northern Ireland
Capital city	London
Population	58.9 million

Language	English, Welsh and Gaelic
Business environment index (10 maximum)	8.45

Information and communication technologies

Telephone mainlines	
Per 1,000 people	588
In largest city (per 1,000 people)	–
Cost of local call (per 3 minutes)	£0.10
Mobile phones (per 1,000 people)	770
International communications	
Cost of call to USA (per 3 minutes)	£0.62
ICT expenditures	
Total ICT	£77,130 million
ICT as % of Gross Domestic Product (GDP)	9.7%
ICT business and government environment (ratings from 1 to 7; 7 is highest/best)	
Broadband internet access availability	5.3
Local specialized IT services availability	6.0
Competition in Internet Service Providers (ISPs)	5.6
Government online services availability	5.5
Laws relating to ICT use	5.2
Government prioritization of ICT	4.9

BRAZIL

Brazil is a country of staggering beauty with stretches of unexplored rainforest, islands with pristine tropical beaches and endless rivers. Roughly the size of the USA (excluding Alaska), Brazil is a vast country encompassing nearly half of South America and bordering most of the continent's other nations. After 40 years of internal migration and population growth, Brazil is also an urban country with more than two out of every three Brazilians living in the city. Brazilian culture has been shaped not only by the Portuguese, who gave the country its most common religion (Catholicism) and language, but also by the country's native Indians, the considerable African population and other settlers from Europe, the Middle East and Asia.

The 2002 presidential election moved Brazil's political agenda to the left when the Workers Party candidate Luiz Inacio 'Lula' da Silva won 61 per cent of the vote. Lula secured the vote by promising to curb hunger and create jobs. Although there have been improvements in education, land reform and welfare, poverty is still widespread and Brazil suffers from urban overcrowding, corruption, environmental abuse and a poor health service.

FACTS AND FIGURES

Full country name	Federative Republic of Brazil
Capital city	Brasilia
Population	175 million
Language	Portuguese; English and French are spoken as second languages

Country risk score (100 = most risky)	50
Business environment index (10 maximum)	6.48

Information and communication technologies

Telephone mainlines	
Per 1,000 people	218
In largest city (per 1,000 people)	311
Cost of local call (per 3 minutes)	£0.02
Mobile phones (per 1,000 people)	167
International communications	
Cost of call to USA (per 3 minutes)	£1.00
ICT expenditures	
Total ICT	£28,017 million
ICT as % of GDP	8.3%
ICT business and government environment	
(ratings from 1 to 7; 7 is highest/best)	
Broadband internet access availability	4.1
Local specialized IT services availability	5.6
Competition in ISPs	5.0
Government online services availability	5.6
Laws relating to ICT use	3.8
Government prioritization of ICT	4.5

Offshore IT services industry

In terms of geographic size and population, Brazil is one of the world's major countries yet it has not developed an IT services industry capable of competing on a global scale. The IT sector suffered through years of protectionist government policies, when Brazilian companies were not able to compete worldwide. Markets were opened up in the mid-1990s and this led to a growth in offshore software services, which by 2002–03 had reached £56 million. Software imports (mainly from the USA) are now estimated to be £672 million each year and this is expected to increase to £3.4 billion by 2005.

Brazil has a large internal IT sector but, although there are hundreds of software companies, most are very small and employ only a few hundred staff. There are some 158,000 IT professionals in Brazil, with 15,000 new entrants each year. Only a small proportion of Brazil's programmers currently work for the offshore IT services industry. The average annual salary for a programmer ranges from £3,400 to £5,500. The main languages are Spanish and Portuguese and English is not widely spoken, which is a disadvantage on the world stage.

Government support for the IT industry has favoured the domestic market and put Brazilian companies at a disadvantage in global markets. A government agency called SOFTEX was set up in 1992 to foster software development and increase software exports. Its main aims included encouraging the creation of new companies in the export sector, developing infrastructure and promoting international trade.

Brazilian software companies are concentrated in the south-east of the country around Sao Paulo and Rio de Janeiro. There are two major industry associations, ABES and ASSESPRO, which promote the software services sector and lobby the government. They have had limited success at an international level and have not always cooperated effectively.

Company profile

Vetta Technologies

Vetta Technologies provides software consulting and outsourced development services. The company has three independent divisions: software engineering, research and development, and quality and process. Offshore customers include Biomind and Proteometrics in the USA and in Europe the French company Alstom and Zagope of Portugal. Vetta's team are all graduates with a high proportion of MScs and PhDs. The focus is on open platforms such as Java and Linux.

www.vettatech.com.

Further information

- **Brazilian Association of Software Companies (ABES)**, www.abes.org.br (Portuguese language only).
- **Association of the Brazilian Companies of Software and IT Services (ASSESPRO)**, www.assespro-sp.org.br (Portuguese language only).
- **Society for IT and Telecommunications Users – Sao Paulo (Sucesu-SP)**, www.sucesusp.org.br (Portuguese language only).

BULGARIA

Bulgaria has changed rapidly since the fall of communism but is still struggling to achieve social and economic stability. In the second half of the 20th century, Bulgaria was one of the most prosperous countries in Eastern Europe, with farmers allowed to till small private plots and industrial growth eventually contributing to over half the GDP. The transition to democracy since 1989 has been difficult, with the renamed Communist Party (now the Bulgarian Socialist Party) maintaining control over the direction taken by the country.

In June 2001, the Bulgarian monarchy made an unprecedented comeback when former king Simeon II was elected prime minister and the Turkish minority was represented in government for the first time. Today the coalition between the Simeon II National Movement and the mainly ethnic Turkish Movement for Rights and Freedoms is unpopular and divided but may yet serve a full term until 2005. The policy focus is on EU accession requirements and completing major privatizations.

Bulgarian is a South Slav language written in the Cyrillic alphabet and remains a strong bond between Bulgarians and Russians. Russian is the second language for older Bulgarians, but younger people are more likely to be interested in speaking English. Bulgarians shake their heads Indian-style to mean yes and nod to mean no.

FACTS AND FIGURES

Full country name	Republic of Bulgaria
Capital city	Sofia
Population	7.9 million
Language	Bulgarian; Turkish is spoken by the ethnic minorities
Country risk score (100 = most risky)	41
Business environment index (10 maximum)	6.18

Information and communication technologies

Telephone mainlines	
Per 1,000 people	359
In largest city (per 1,000 people)	564
Cost of local call (per 3 minutes)	£0.01
Mobile phones (per 1,000 people)	191
International communications	
Cost of call to USA (per 3 minutes)	£1.33
ICT expenditures	
Total ICT	£297 million
ICT as % of GDP	3.8%
ICT business and government environment (ratings from 1 to 7; 7 is highest/best)	
Broadband internet access availability	2.9
Local specialized IT services availability	4.3
Competition in ISPs	3.7
Government online services availability	3.0
Laws relating to ICT use	3.3
Government prioritization of ICT	3.6

Offshore IT services industry

The offshore industry in Bulgaria focuses on application development, product development and application maintenance services. Exports are around £45 million each year. Highly trained software professionals earn average first-year salaries that range from £2,000 to £3,400.

More than 100 representatives of Bulgarian and foreign companies and partner organizations took part in 'Bulgarian IT Day' at the world's largest ICT exhibition – CeBIT in Hannover, Germany – in March 2004. The Deputy Prime Minister and Minister of Transport and Communications, Nikolay Vassilev launched the Bulgarian initiative, in its third appearance at CeBIT. The exhibit promoted the talent available within Bulgaria using the slogan ICTalent.

Company profile

iConcepts

iConcepts has its headquarters in Philadelphia and maintains development centres in Sofia, Bulgaria and Moscow. The Company's core strengths are strong software capabilities, data acquisition, web-based archiving and information distribution. Its strategic partner NETtelcos is a Virginia-based hosting provider and ISP specializing in secure, high-volume and ultra-redundant systems. iConcepts provides custom solutions for a wide range of businesses and industries, including electronic archiving systems, data acquisition systems that feature cutting edge index, search and retrieval functions and information dissemination systems. The solutions use a wide range of technologies, platforms and operating systems such as .NET, Java, PDA, Windows, Microsoft CE, PocketPC, PalmOS and Mac.

Visit www.iconcepts-inc.com for more information.

Further information

- The **Bulgarian Association of Information Technologies (BAIT)** is the largest and most influential IT sector organization in Bulgaria. Formed in 1995, it currently has over 150 members. BAIT's mission is to define and defend the common interests of its members, by establishing IT as a priority in the development of the national economy. The association works actively with the government and legislative organizations to devise national IT policy and develop egovernment strategy. BAIT organizes the two largest annual high-tech exhibitions in Bulgaria – BAIT EXPO (in October) and BAIT Internet EXPO and Telecomex (in April). See www.bait.bg.
- The **InvestBulgaria Agency** is a government agency providing assistance and support to investors. See investbg.government.bg

CANADA

Situated between the Atlantic and Pacific oceans, Canada is the world's second largest country (Russia is first). It enjoys an incredible mix of native flora and fauna, comprising eight vegetation zones, most of which are dominated by forest. English and French are the two official languages though the French spoken in Canada is a dialect known as Quebecois. The French influence on Quebec can be seen in architecture, music, food and religion.

The 1950s saw a huge wave of European immigration to Canada, followed in the 1960s by a further influx of Asians, Arabs, Indians, Italians, Hispanics and Caribbeans. The post-war era was a period of economic expansion and prosperity. Since 1975 a series of land rights agreements has been signed with Canada's native peoples, giving them some control over vast swathes of the northern part of the country.

The resentment felt by French-speaking Quebec towards English-speaking Canada reached a climax in 1995 when the country came close to breaking up. Current concerns include maintaining social programmes, high taxes and national security in the wake of terrorist attacks on the USA.

FACTS AND FIGURES

Full country name	Canada
Capital city	Ottawa
Population	31.4 million
Language	English, French
Business environment index (10 maximum)	8.65

Information and communication technologies

Telephone mainlines	
Per 1,000 people	676
In largest city (per 1,000 people)	–
Cost of local call (per 3 minutes)	–
Mobile phones (per 1,000 people)	362
International communications	
Cost of call to USA (per 3 minutes)	£0.67
ICT expenditures	
Total ICT	£34,102 million
ICT as % of GDP	8.7%
ICT Business and government environment (ratings from 1 to 7; 7 is highest/best)	
Broadband internet access availability	6.0
Local specialized IT services availability	5.7
Competition in ISPs	6.1

Government online services availability	5.6
Laws relating to ICT use	5.1
Government prioritization of ICT	5.3

Offshore IT services industry

The outsourcing industry in Canada has developed as a safe near-shore option for American companies and exports £2,000 billion worth of software and computer services each year. Canada's advantages include lower salary costs, political stability, the widespread use of English, and the proximity of major cities to the USA. The only significant risk is that exchange rate fluctuations can erode savings in salary costs. Canada benefits from the lowest software manufacturing costs in any G7 country – the average IT salary is around £20,000 annually. As it cannot compete on price with the low-cost programmers in, for example, India and the Philippines, Canada generally focuses on higher-value design and development work for other countries. The industry has particular strengths in application development, business intelligence software, customer relationship management systems, digital and multimedia software, internet and ecommerce.

The industry in Canada is very dependent on the American market with over 80 per cent of IT products and services exported to the USA. Canada's top two outsourcing software services exporters are IBM and EDS. Most of Canada's IT services exports are from American firms exporting back into the USA. Canada benefits from the trading alliance created by the North America Free Trade Act (NAFTA) between the USA, Canada and Mexico. This trade zone permits the free flow of people, goods and services between the three countries and provides a compatible legal framework for the protection of property in all three countries. The Canadian government offers tax breaks for IT-related exports.

The IT industry in Canada is focused around Toronto (financial services, software development and mainframe technology), Ottawa (wireless and semiconductor technology and software development) and Vancouver (software development). There is a strong focus on quality, with many companies meeting ISO standards and many having CMM initiatives.

There are 240,000 IT professionals working in Canada with 6,000 new software engineers qualifying each year. A relatively liberal immigration policy has encouraged skilled software professionals to move into Canada from around the world, maintaining the large pool of skilled resources.

Company profiles

CGI

CGI employs around 25,000 professionals and is the largest Canadian independent IT services firm and the fifth largest in North America. The company provides end-to-end IT and business process services to clients worldwide, using a customized delivery model that combines onsite and offsite operations. In June 2004 outsourcing comprised about 60 per cent of CGI's business and some 38 per cent of its clients were based outside Canada. The company has over 25 years experience in outsourcing, applications management, consulting and systems integration. In 1994, CGI became the first IT company in North America to be ISO 9001 certified for its Project Management Framework. In 2002, CGI's India operations achieved a CMM Level 5 rating for its ability to focus the entire organization on continuous process improvement.

Visit www.cgi.com for more information.

Keane

Boston-based Keane offers business consulting, application development, integration and management outsourcing services. Its subsidiary, Keane Canada, is based in Toronto. Services are provided through an integrated network of branch offices in North America and the UK, and Advanced Development Centres (ADCs) in the USA, Canada and India. This global service delivery model offers customers the flexibility and economic advantage of fluidly allocating work between a variety of delivery options including onsite at the customer's offices or offsite at a remote location, either near-shore in Halifax, Nova Scotia or offshore in India. The Halifax ADC has been serving Fortune 500 clients since 1997 and has been independently assessed at CMM Level 5.

Visit www.keane.com/offshore/canada for more information.

Further information

The **Information Technology Association of Canada (ITAC)** is the voice of the Canadian ICT industry. With its affiliated organizations across the country, ITAC represents 1,300 companies in the ICT industry in all sectors including the production of hardware, microelectronics, software and electronic content and the delivery of IT services. The association's network of companies accounts for more than 70 per cent of the sector. See www.itac.ca.

CHINA

The third largest country in the world, China is bounded to the north by the deserts of Mongolia, to the west by the inhospitable Tibetan plateau and the Himalayas, and to the east by the East and South China seas. China's 22 provinces and 5 autonomous regions are governed from Beijing, along with some 5,000 islands. Hong Kong and Macau have been returned to China and form Special Administrative Regions. Disputed territories are found off the south-east coast, Taiwan being the best known.

Since the 1990s, the Chinese communist leadership has charted a new course based on economic growth and modernization. Problems remain with continued civil rights abuses, corruption and a stagnant rural economy, but membership of the World Trade Organization is a big step forward. China's legislature, the National People's Congress, approved more than a dozen changes to the state constitution in March 2004, including protection of private property, human rights and land rights.

FACTS AND FIGURES

Full country name	People's Republic of China
Capital city	Beijing
Population	1,281 million
Language	Putonghua or Mandarin is the national language; other principal dialects include Cantonese or Yue and Shangainese or Wu, minority languages include Tibetan and Mongolian
Country risk score (100 = most risky)	42
Business environment index (10 maximum)	6.23

Information and communication technologies

Telephone mainlines	
Per 1,000 people	137
In largest city (per 1,000 people)	584
Cost of local call (per 3 minutes)	–
Mobile phones (per 1,000 people)	110
International communications	
Cost of call to USA (per 3 minutes)	£3.75
ICT expenditures	
Total ICT	£37,303 million
ICT as % of GDP	5.7%
ICT business and government environment (ratings from 1 to 7; 7 is highest/best)	
Broadband internet access availability	2.9
Local specialized IT services availability	4.3
Competition in ISPs	3.7
Government online services availability	3.5
Laws relating to ICT use	3.5
Government prioritization of ICT	5.3

Offshore IT services industry

China could potentially challenge India as the dominant country in the global offshore services industry. The outsourced software services sector currently earns about £840 million each year with an annual growth rate of 30 per cent. China has a large supply of qualified IT professionals and the government is committed to the development of the IT industry, but the country is held back by the immaturity of the domestic market, a lack of rigorous intellectual property protection in practice and insufficient entrepreneurial and managerial skills.

Chinese organizations have not implemented the large-scale, complex enterprise systems that are commonplace in the USA and Western Europe and so Chinese IT professionals have not been able to develop expertise in planning and managing major IT projects. Most Chinese programmers focus on low-level coding and maintenance. There are some 400,000 IT professionals in China, with about 50,000 new graduates each year, but there is a shortage of high-level system architects, designers and project managers. University courses continue to emphasize traditional engineering fields and, as a result, Chinese programmers tend to lack the expertise needed for systems analysis and software design.

Wage rates are low – the average annual salary for a Chinese programmer is about £4,500 annually. For the past nine years, English has been taught in schools and students have had to pass a proficiency test, so Chinese professionals can read and write English, but do not necessarily speak it well. English-speaking programmers command higher salaries of about £5,100 annually.

The government has identified the IT industry as a critical growth area and has decided that China should become a world technology leader. A number of initiatives have been launched to support and build the industry. The Five Year plan (for 2001–05) includes a target growth of more than 30 per cent annually, which would result in a market of £11 billion by 2005. The China Ministry of Science and Technology established the Torch Centre, a high-tech development programme and in 2003 launched the China Offshore Software Engineering Project (COSEP). A number of Chinese software companies from regional software parks will be selected to go through a training programme supervised by an American company, ExperExchange. Once this is successfully completed, Chinese companies will receive the official seal of approval from the government, which guarantees to potential clients that they have the necessary processes in place to tackle complex outsourced projects. The government has also encouraged partnerships and joint ventures with foreign companies and introduced various tax incentives and exemptions from regulations to promote the software industry. Software piracy remains a major concern, despite some well-publicized campaigns by the government and the establishment of the first copyright registration agency.

Over recent years there has been massive investment in the telecommunications infrastructure, with significant growth in the mobile phone market and increased internet connection speeds. Services in rural areas remain poor, but telecommunications links in the major urban areas are improving.

Chinese companies have not yet developed a reputation for reliability and quality services. Some companies have achieved ISO 9000 certification and a number of firms have reached CMM Level 3. The software industry is based around Beijing, Shanghai and Guangdong along the east coast of China, where most of the leading research institutions and universities are also found. There are 19 software parks across China in which over 2,000 companies are located. The Chinese industry specializes in embedded software, wireless technology and open source software.

Company profiles

Neusoft

Neusoft is one of the leading software and solution companies in China, and originated from the Northeastern University in 1991. The company focuses on three main businesses: software services, education and training, and digital medical products. Neosoft has about 6,000 employees and offices in 40 Chinese cities, the USA, Japan and Hong Kong. It has established four development and service centres — the Neusoft Parks in Shenyang, Dalian, Nanhai and Chengdu.

Visit www.neusoft.com for more information.

Microsoft

Microsoft opened its first offices in China in 1992. The Microsoft China Research and Development Centre opened in Beijing in 1995 and has more than 150 employees – it is one of the largest foreign-owned software research and development centres in China. The Microsoft Global Technical Support Centre in Shanghai employs over 400 people to support customers worldwide. 'Microsoft is very pleased to be partnering with the Chinese government and industry to develop its software industry', Bill Gates said during a visit to China in 2003. 'Building on a strong base of talent and skills in its software sector, the momentum of Chinese enterprises in the use of information technologies, and strong government support, China has great potential to realize its potential as a global leader in software.'

Microsoft has strategic partnerships with several Chinese organizations including Xi Ji Group and the Industrial and Commercial Bank of China.

Visit www.microsoft.com for more information.

Further information

- The **Hong Kong Information Technology Federation (HKITF)** was founded in 1980 as a non-profit, non-political trade association to provide a forum for the IT industry in Hong Kong. It has over 300 members and promotes local IT firms through activities such as exhibitions, seminars and after-office-hours Networking Hours. See www.hkitf.org.hk.

- **China Software Industry Association (CSIA)**, www.csia.org.cn (Chinese language only).
- **Ministry of Information Industry (MII)**, www.mii.gov.cn (Chinese language only).

THE CZECH REPUBLIC

The Czech Republic came into being in 1993 when Czechoslovakia split into two. Prague became the capital with Vaclav Havel, who had negotiated the communist government's resignation in 1989, elected as first president. Thanks to stringent economic policies, booming tourism and a solid industrial base, the Czech Republic is seeing a strong recovery. Unemployment is negligible, shops are full and many cities are getting facelifts. Problems remain, however, with a shortage of affordable housing, steeply rising crime, severe pollution, a deteriorating health system and occasional political instability. The current governing coalition, led by the Czech Social Democratic Party has won parliamentary approval for a fiscal reform package but is weakened by political in-fighting.

The Czech Republic's architecture includes some of the finest Baroque and Art Nouveau buildings in Europe. The Czechs have also excelled at other art forms such as illuminated manuscripts, religious sculpture and marionette and puppet theatre.

FACTS AND FIGURES

Full country name	Czech Republic
Capital city	Prague
Population	10.2 million
Language	Czech. German and Slovak widely spoken; both Russian and English are taught at schools as second languages
Country risk score (100 = most risky)	33
Business environment index (10 maximum)	7.30

Information and communication technologies

Telephone mainlines	
Per 1,000 people	375
In largest city (per 1,000 people)	666
Cost of local call (per 3 minutes)	£0.06

Mobile phones (per 1,000 people)	675
International communications	
Cost of call to USA (per 3 minutes)	£0.44
ICT expenditures	
Total ICT	£2,774 million
ICT as % of GDP	9.5%
ICT business and government environment	
(ratings from 1 to 7; 7 is highest/best)	
Broadband internet access availability	4.3
Local specialized IT services availability	5.5
Competition in ISPs	5.5
Government online services availability	4.5
Laws relating to ICT use	4.2
Government prioritization of ICT	4.8

Offshore IT services industry

The IT services industry in the Czech Republic has seen significant growth based on the well-educated workforce, government support and a good telecommunications infrastructure. There is a high level of general education in the country, with a particular emphasis on science and technical students. There are over 45,000 students at 7 universities, the largest of which is Prague CVUT, Europe's second oldest technical university, teaching more than 17,000 students.

There are a number of corporate research centres in the country including ON Semiconductor's Design Centre, Rockwell Automation's Independent Advanced Technical Laboratory and Honeywell's Research and Development Centre in Prague developing control software and tools. The offshore software services market amounts to around £45 million each year. The country's core competences are application development, product development and application maintenance.

The Czech Republic offers subsidies to UK businesses to relocate their IT services to the country. CzechInvest, the government's foreign investment agency, will cover up to 50 per cent of investment costs for firms that relocate software development, call centres and IT outsourcing centres. Company law in the Czech Republic is not up to western standards – it can take nearly three months to set up a company and nine years to complete a liquidation. CzechInvest is used to overcoming such problems. 'I think we have to deal with the problems that we have,' chief executive Martin Jahn told the BBC. 'We are very open about the room for improvement that we have in our business legislation. I don't think that the situation is much worse here than in neighbouring countries' (news.bbc.co.uk).

Company profile

DHL

DHL is the largest logistics company in the world, operating through its affiliates and agents in all continents of the world. The company has nearly 170,000 employees in 228 countries. As part of a consolidation of internal functions, DHL decided to open a new IT shared services centre in Prague covering the whole of Europe. Most of DHL's IT activities in Great Britain and Switzerland are being moved to Prague where 400 high quality jobs have been created. This is expected to increase to 1,000 by the end of 2005 when Prague will become the largest technology centre in DHL's network. 'Wage costs in the Czech Republic are one third of those in Western European countries. Even after the country joins the European Union and wages increase they will not exceed two thirds of the Western European level,' according to Stephen McGuckin, global chief information officer of DHL. 'We ultimately chose the Czech Republic for its availability of a skilled and flexible labour force, well established and reliable telecommunications networks, good air links as well as for the optimum incentives package offered by the Czech government, which was mediated by the Ministry of Industry and Trade.'

Visit www.dhl.com for further information (additional material from www.czechinvest.org).

Further information

- **CzechInvest** describes itself as the investment gateway to the Czech Republic. It mediated supplier contracts for Czech companies (in all sectors) in 2003 worth £12 million. CzechInvest administers an expanding database of Czech suppliers who are interested in long-term cooperation with foreign investors. See www.czechinvest.org.
- **Association for Consulting to Business**, www.asocpor.cz (Czech language only).

HUNGARY

After the collapse of communism, the country became the Republic of Hungary in 1989 and later held free elections – the first in more than four decades. Despite initial success in curbing inflation and lowering interest rates, a host of economic problems has slowed the pace of development. Hungary joined the North Atlantic Treaty Organization (NATO) in 1999 and the EU in 2004.

The centre-left governing coalition looks set to serve out its term, which runs to mid-2006. Excessive wage rises in 2002–03 sustained growth but have contributed to the return of high fiscal and external debts. Given stubbornly high fiscal deficits and reawakening inflation, monetary policy is likely to remain tight in the medium term.

Hungarian art and architecture show Romanesque, Gothic, Baroque and Art Nouveau influences. The country has one of the finest folk traditions in Europe, producing excellent examples of embroidery, pottery, ceiling and wall painting, and objects carved from wood or bone. Hungarians tend to have a sceptical view of faith and some have speculated that this is why they have a high success rate in science and mathematics.

FACTS AND FIGURES

Full country name	Republic of Hungary
Capital city	Budapest
Population	10.2 million
Language	Hungarian (Magyar); Russian and English are taught in schools as second languages
Country risk score (100 = most risky)	36
Business environment index (10 maximum)	7.14

Information and communication technologies

Telephone mainlines	
Per 1,000 people	374
In largest city (per 1,000 people)	588
Cost of local call (per 3 minutes)	£0.05
Mobile phones (per 1,000 people)	498
International communications	
Cost of call to USA (per 3 minutes)	£0.55
ICT expenditures	
Total ICT	£2,602 million
ICT as % of GDP	8.9%
ICT business and government environment (ratings from 1 to 7; 7 is highest/best)	
Broadband internet access availability	4.2
Local specialized IT services availability	5.1
Competition in ISPs	4.3
Government online services availability	4.4
Laws relating to ICT use	4.9
Government prioritization of ICT	5.4

Offshore IT services industry

Lying in the centre of Europe, Hungary is ideally located to serve both emerging and established markets. Its population is among the best educated in the region with excellent universities and a fast-growing reputation as a research and development centre of excellence.

Hungary's government is one of the most supportive in Eastern Europe in encouraging the development of the software services sector. Its initiatives include tax incentives to encourage firms to provide IT equipment to workers, a partnership with small businesses to support IT training, support for the introduction of broadband networks and job creation subsidies to encourage training for the unemployed in basic IT skills. The country has a good telecommunications infrastructure, resulting from a large investment over the past decade.

The IT market in Hungary is more mature and is growing rather more slowly than other countries in the region, but IT, management and entrepreneurial skills are more widely available. Application development, product development and application maintenance services are the core competences offered. Offshore software exports amount to some £45 million annually. The ICT sector as a whole is currently growing at around 10 per cent each year and represents about 12 per cent of GDP.

Company profile

Hungarian Software Alliance

The Hungarian Software Alliance (HSA) was formed in 2002 by 12 of the top 100 Hungarian software companies. Development sites are based near leading Hungarian universities and provide a range of IT services such as data capture, call centres and portal developments. HSA also creates dedicated offshore development centres for clients.

Visit www.h-s-a.hu for more information.

Further information

- The **Hungarian Association of Information Technology Companies (IVSZ)** aims to positively influence the progress of the information society by identifying and progressing key issues such as the question of trust in ecommerce, the acceptance and use of digital signatures and access to the internet. IVSZ has over 260 members who employ nearly 30,000 professionals and account for 85 per cent of the Hungarian ICT market. See www.ivsz.hu.
- The **Hungarian Investment and Trade Development Agency** provides complementary investment strategy consulting and comprehensive business services through its extensive network of Hungarian and international offices. See www.itdh.hu.

INDIA

India is the seventh largest country in the world and is bordered by Pakistan to the north-west, China, Nepal and Bhutan to the north, and Bangladesh and Myanmar to the east. The borders with Pakistan and China have long been disputed, but peaceful agreement with China has been reached on establishing the border along the Indian state of Sikkim and the Pakistan peace process is now on track. Cricket matches between India and Pakistan have even resumed.

Following years of economic depression and isolation when foreign exports and imports were strictly controlled, Rajiv Ghandi of the Congress Party was the first leader to encourage foreign investment and the use of modern technology. He was prime minister between 1984 and 1989. When the Congress Party returned to power in 1991, Rajiv Ghandi was dead and the leadership passed to Narasimha Rao. It was Rao who introduced major economic reform and, together with his finance minister Manmohan Singh, devalued the rupee, dismantled trade barriers and reduced bureaucracy. The Bharatiya Janata Party (BJP), which came to power in 1996, adopted a more traditionalist Hindu stance but also continued the economic reforms, particularly in its support for the ICT industry. The BJP gained popular support within India for its nuclear weapons tests in 1998.

The Congress Party won India's month-long parliamentary elections in 2004 and former finance minister Manmohan Singh was named prime minister. The ruling United Progressive Alliance (UPA) coalition depends on the support of communist and other left-wing parties.

After expanding by an estimated 8.3 per cent in 2003–04, GDP will grow slightly more slowly at 7.3 per cent in 2004–05 because of a smaller harvest and weaker growth in personal incomes. The trade deficit will remain large, but will be offset by surpluses on services. The Indian rupee is expected to continue to rise against the US dollar for most of 2004, but to depreciate in 2005.

There is no 'Indian' language as such – 18 languages are officially recognized by the constitution, but over 1,600 minor languages and dialects were listed in the 1991 census. English is widely spoken by the wealthy and educated and is seen as a passport to the world of international business. But less than 5 per cent of the total population have proficiency in English.

FACTS AND FIGURES

Full country name	Republic of India
Capital city	New Delhi
Population	1,048 million
Language	Hindi and English are the official languages; over 1,600 languages and dialects are spoken throughout India
Country risk score (100 = most risky)	39
Business environment index (10 maximum)	6.15

> *Information and communication technologies*
>
> **Telephone mainlines**
>
> | | |
> |---|---|
> | Per 1,000 people | 38 |
> | In largest city (per 1,000 people) | 136 |
> | Cost of local call (per 3 minutes) | £0.01 |
> | Mobile phones (per 1,000 people) | 6 |
>
> **International communications**
>
> | | |
> |---|---|
> | Cost of call to USA (per 3 minutes) | £1.79 |
>
> **ICT expenditures**
>
> | | |
> |---|---|
> | Total ICT | £11,011 million |
> | ICT as % of GDP | 3.9% |
>
> **ICT business and government environment**
> (ratings from 1 to 7; 7 is highest/best)
>
> | | |
> |---|---|
> | Broadband internet access availability | 3.2 |
> | Local specialized IT services availability | 5.8 |
> | Competition in ISPs | 4.5 |
> | Government online services availability | 3.9 |
> | Laws relating to ICT use | 4.3 |
> | Government prioritization of ICT | 5.6 |

Offshore IT services industry

India is the undisputed leader of the global offshore services industry and sets the benchmark against which all other countries are measured. The scale, professionalism and commitment shown by the major Indian suppliers (and many of the medium-sized firms too) are very impressive. Although now facing competition from China, Russia and elsewhere, India retains some compelling competitive advantages in the global marketplace:

- It has the advantage of the first mover, the leader in the global growth of offshore services.
- In NASSCOM, it has an enthusiastic and effective trade association that influences government and promotes the industry overseas.
- Education is highly valued and the universities and colleges provide large numbers of graduates each year.
- There is a focus on quality processes, with Indian companies achieving much higher levels of compliance with internationally recognized standards than is commonly seen in other countries, including the UK and USA.
- The Indian government recognized early on that IT is an area where the country could potentially have a major global influence and boost its own economy. Continuing support from both central and state governments underpins the success of the offshore services industry.

The IT services industry began to develop in India in the 1990s, when Indian firms competed with companies like IBM and EDS on the basis of low labour costs. Revenue grew rapidly by over 50 per cent each year from 1994 until 2001. As the technology bubble burst in 2001, expenditure on IT services around the world fell. The outsourcing market in India had been expected to grow by 40 per cent in 2001, but the increase was only 20 per cent (www.economist.com). In a masterstroke, the Indian IT services industry saw this as an opportunity to prepare for a future upturn. Low-cost services conjure up an image of shoddy work and poor quality. India tackled this head on. Investments in software development centres and recruitment were frozen. India developed its own brand as an outsourcing location able to offer services that equalled any available from the leading multinational companies. Indian firms invested in training and achieved compliance with the highest international quality standards. As a result, India was in an excellent position to take advantage of the renewed worldwide focus on outsourcing as companies looked to reduce costs during the global economic downturn. It is often said that companies go to India for the lower costs, but stay for the quality of service and productivity levels.

India currently exports £5.6 billion of software and IT services each year, including sales of £1 billion to Western Europe. The market is growing at about 30 per cent annually. By 2008 NASSCOM predicts that export earnings will exceed £28 billion with total sales in the IT industry amounting to some £49 billion. The IT industry will then account for some 25 per cent of all India's exports and about 8 per cent of GDP, but this wealth will be generated by just 0.25 per cent of the population (www.computing.co.uk). Although the larger offshore companies have survived the global economic downturn, smaller firms have not always been so successful. The market is going through a period of consolidation, with the larger companies growing and themselves expanding overseas, setting up development centres in Eastern Europe, South America and the Far East.

At the heart of the success of the Indian industry lies its strong focus on quality management and processes. All the top-tier Indian suppliers are certified at CMM Level 5, in fact Prabhuu Sinha, senior vice president of Satyam Computer Services, told me that some 75 per cent of all the companies certified at Level 5 in the world are based in India.

Reflecting the importance of the industry to its economy, the government has appointed a Minister for Information Technology. A crucial early decision by the Ministry was not to regulate the market. The government provides a comprehensive package of tax incentives, encourages foreign ownership of IT companies and is progressing telecommunications deregulation to support the sector. In a country where bureaucracy is renown for causing delay, the government understands the importance of getting things done quickly to the well-being of the IT industry.

The copyright of computer software is protected under the provisions of the Indian Copyright Act 1957. Major changes to this law were introduced in 1994 and came into effect in 1995. These amendments introduced for the first time in India a clear explanation of the rights of the copyright holder, the position on software rentals, the rights of the user to make back-up copies, and punishments and fines for infringement of software copyright. The Information Technology Act of 2000 was the first attempt to regulate the IT industry to prevent hacking, identity theft and so on.

Tighter data protection and privacy measures are being developed and look likely to be introduced by the end of 2004. Rather than propose a separate law, the government is considering an amendment to the Information Technology Act of 2000. NASSCOM is helping to develop the new clauses. The original act covers only unauthorized access and data theft from computers and networks and has no provisions relating to data privacy. The new clauses are being designed to meet EU data protection requirements and the USA Safe Harbor privacy principles. Once the revised legislation is in place India plans to negotiate with the EU for recognition as a country that offers an adequate level of protection for personal data.

The government has been actively challenging the backlash in the UK and elsewhere, putting the case for the use of offshore outsourcing to increase competitiveness in a global marketplace and the need for the resources that India can offer. At an EU and India business summit in November 2003, Indian Prime Minister Atal Bihari Vajpayee said, 'The demographic profile of Europe and America necessarily means that these countries will need the induction of a younger workforce from outside in the coming decades' (www.computerworld.com).

The India Business Group (IBG) is an informal organization created at the initiative of the Indian High Commissioner in 1999. The Group brings together senior executives and professionals from Indian companies in the UK and also leading consultants and solicitors from British firms who advise clients on doing business in India and the UK. The IBG hopes to convince the UK government that British companies need to be able to exploit the potential savings that can be made through offshore outsourcing to remain globally competitive. The Group has joined an industry panel that advises the UK government on work permit policy (www.hcilondon.net/business-information).

Every year in India more than 2 million students graduate and of these 80 per cent speak English. About 280,000 software engineers graduate and another 300,000 diploma engineers gain their qualifications. India possesses good public and private universities, many of which are recognized as among the global leaders in education. These include the prestigious seven Indian Institutes of Technology and four Institutes of

Management, each year producing 3,500 graduates and 2,000 MBA graduates respectively. Further strengthening the Indian education system, training institutes such as NIIT and APTECH have developed to provide software training throughout India. These institutes provide opportunities for trainee programmers to learn, practice and gain certified qualifications in applications produced by Microsoft, Oracle and other foreign companies. Although well placed in terms of new recruits, the challenge for India is the current shortage of middle and senior-level managers. Another concern is that a NASSCOM survey in February 2003 predicted that the supply of new graduates will not be able to keep up with demand and there will be a shortfall of 250,000 by 2008 (www.silicon.news).

Wage levels for Indian software engineers are much lower than in the UK, but they are higher than salaries for Chinese and Philippine programmers. The average Indian IT programmer earns from £3,500 to £6,700 annually. An IT professional with three to five years' programming experience can earn £14,600. Salaries have risen as competition between the offshore companies for the best talent intensifies.

Although the telecommunications industry in India is deregulated there is at present little competition with the market dominated by three state-owned companies. Service and reliability varies across the country. Within the IT parks, telecommunications and power services are very reliable and well supported, with in-built spare capacity as standard. Outside these areas, the infrastructure is not so dependable and service disruptions should be expected. Recent months have seen a rapid growth in mobile phone penetration in India. NASSCOM estimates that mobile phone demand reached 33 million in 2003–04 and will increase further to 49 million in 2004–05. Looking ahead, NASSCOM has expressed concern about a potential shortage of international bandwidth. Their estimates suggest that demand will exceed supply by 20 Gbps in mid-2005.

The main centres of the offshore industry are in Bangalore, Chennai, Delhi, Hyderabad, Kolkata (formerly Calcutta), Mumbai (formerly Bombay) and Pune. Over the past six years there has been a tremendous growth in the technology parks established in India and geared towards the requirements of the knowledge industry. Located in key areas such as Chennai and Bangalore, these parks offer Silicon Valley-type infrastructure. Multi-tenanted 'intelligent' buildings, custom-built facilities and large sprawling campuses are tailored to meet customer requirements.

Indian offshore IT services companies are increasingly developing into global players, themselves looking offshore from India, moving work around the world to mitigate the risk of over-dependency on any one location and to maintain the most competitive prices for their services. The average contract signed by Indian companies is increasing in value – NASSCOM has reported that in 2003 there was a 60 per cent increase over

2002. The average contract is now worth over £2 million and is increasingly likely to be multi-year, signalling a longer-term customer relationship.

The offshore industry is striving to move from a technology focus to a more service-oriented approach. In the past, a lack of business skills and industry-specific expertise has held India back from the higher-value IT consulting market. Indian companies have seen the IT department as their client rather than senior business executives. This could change as the Indian market develops. In a sort of role reversal, some Indian companies are expanding into America. Wipro has purchased two small American consultancies and two Indian conglomerates, the Godrej Group and the Essar Group, have each bought an American call centre. This is truly a global industry.

Company profiles

Cognizant Technology Solutions

With its headquarters in New Jersey, Cognizant Technology Solutions operates an offshore organization that is rated one of India's top employers. It provides application management, development and integration services, infrastructure management, business process outsourcing and related services through its onsite/offshore model. The company has more than 12,000 employees and development centres in India, Phoenix and Ireland. It maintains assessments company-wide for all its quality initiatives – ISO 9001, CMMI and P-CMM Level 5 and BS 7799. Cognizant announced in December 2003 that it would be expanding its facilities in India and increasing its global head count by 40 per cent in 2004. Campuses in Pune and Chennai will be expanded and a new facility in Bangalore built. The company also has operations in Kolkata (formerly Calcutta) and Hyderabad. Cognizant's 60 per cent earnings growth rate is outstripping its rivals. 'We're growing faster because clients find we're successful at managing large programmes. We can help with redeploying or retraining people and making sure the cost savings are coming through,' chief executive officer, Kumar Mahadera told *Computer Weekly* in 2003. 'We've spent a lot more in the US and Europe to provide consulting groups that can handle change management. We're also the top recruiter from the business schools [in India], and we have a huge number of MBAs.'

Visit www.cognizant.com for more information (additional material from www.computerworld.com and www.computerweekly.co.uk).

HCL Technologies

HCL Technologies is one of India's leading global IT service and product engineering companies, with over 450 clients worldwide and 26 offices in 15 countries. The company currently employs about 15,000 people. Total earnings in 2002–03 were £217 million. Services are delivered through 16 state-of-the-art software development centres in India and include technology development, application services, technology design and business process outsourcing. Six entrepreneurs set-up the company in 1975 and despite the lack of venture capital available in India at that time, opened their first office in the suburbs of New Delhi, naming their business Hindustan Computers Limited in 1976. After eight years, HCL had become the largest computer systems and services company in India. Today, HCL Technologies is a global IT enterprise with headquarters at Noida, India.

Visit www.hcltech.com for more information.

Infosys Technologies

Infosys Technologies provides consulting and IT services to clients globally. Corporate headquarters are in Bangalore and worldwide offices are found in Argentina, Australia, Belgium, Canada, France, Germany, Hong Kong, India, Japan, the Netherlands, Singapore, Sweden, Switzerland, the UK, the United Arab Emirates and the USA. Infosys has over 27,000 employees and first achieved CMMI Level 5 certification in 2002. In April 2004, Infosys announced that its annual earnings had exceeded $1 billion (£560 million) for the first time. The company has nine development centres in India in Bangalore, Hyderabad, Trivandrum, Mysore, Pune, Mohali, Mangalore, Bhuvaneswar and Chennai. Infosys' global headquarters and campus at Electronics City, Bangalore, is the world's single largest software development facility among IT services companies. Global development centres in Chicago, Dallas, San Francisco Bay Area, Boston, Toronto, Tokyo and Croydon expand the capabilities of Infosys' global delivery model to use talent and infrastructure in different parts of the world.

Visit www.infosys.com for more information.

Mastek

Mastek is a global IT application outsourcing company with its headquarters and principal offshore delivery facility based at Mumbai (formerly Bombay). Incorporated in 1982, Mastek's earnings in 2003–04 reached £51 million. The company employs over 2,400 professionals worldwide and was the first IT solutions company in the world to be assessed at Capability Maturity Model (SW-CMM) Level 5 for its software processes and P-CMM Level 3 for its people practices. Mastek has a multinational executive board and wholly owned subsidiaries in the USA, the UK, Singapore, Malaysia, Germany, Belgium and an office in Japan. It provides technical consulting, product integration, customized application development and ongoing application management services, combining onsite and offshore resources to maximize responsiveness while delivering substantial savings.

Visit www.mastek.com for more information.

Satyam Computer Services

Satyam Computer Services is a leading global consulting and IT services company that offers a wide range of solutions in the automotive, banking and financial, insurance and healthcare, manufacturing and other sectors. Over 15,000 IT professionals employed at development centres in India, the USA, the UK, the United Arab Emirates, Canada, Singapore, Malaysia, China, Japan and Australia, serve over 325 global companies. Satyam's marketing network spans 45 countries across 6 continents. It has been assessed at CMM Level 5 and was the first in the world to be ISO 9001:2000 certified. The company was a co-founder of the eServices Capability Model, which was developed in partnership with Carnegie Mellon University. The model guides IT-enabled outsourcing service providers to appraise and improve their capability to provide consistently high-quality services in the networked economy. Satyam's results for 2003–04 showed a 32 per cent year-on-year growth with earnings from software services reaching £310 million. 'Our focus on competency enhancement and relationship management has been a key factor in growing existing accounts as well as acquiring new customers', Chairman B. Ramalinga Raju said, commenting on the results. 'The current customer base, including 101 Fortune Global 500 customers, is indicative of the potential for our growth momentum. We shall continue to invest in sharpening our skills and processes for partnering with them in their journey towards business excellence.'

Visit www.satyam.com for more information.

Tata Consultancy Services

With more than three decades of experience, Tata Consultancy Services (TCS), one of 80 companies in the Tata Group, offers end-to-end strategy consulting and system integration to customers in 55 countries. TCS has 100 offices in 32 countries and employs 24,000 consultants. In 2003 a Gartner study rated TCS the top Indian offshore service provider. Earnings were £582 million in 2002–03. The company follows a continuous quality enhancement process and in August 2004 it was announced that TCS had become the first company in the world to be assessed at CMMI and P-CMM Level 5 enterprise-wide. All of TCS's major development centres are ISO 9001:2000 certified and its quality management system is also ISO 9001:2000 compliant. TCS has services practices in various areas – ebusiness, application development and maintenance, architecture and technology consulting, engineering services, security, large projects, quality consulting, and infrastructure development and management. Clients include General Motors, Ford Motors, Citibank, British Telecom, AXA Insurance, Deutsche Bank and P&O Nedlloyd.

Visit www.tata.com/tcs for more information.

Wipro Technologies

Wipro Technologies is the global technology services division of Wipro Limited and offers software application development and maintenance, IT consulting, business process outsourcing, product design, system integration and remote infrastructure management services. With more than 340 customers across the USA, Europe and Japan, Wipro Technologies employs over 29,000 people from 18 nationalities and operates 8 nearshore development centres, 33 sales offices and one disaster recovery centre. In 2003–04 earnings were £756 million, representing an increase of 36 per cent year on year. Azim Premji, chairman of Wipro, commenting on the results said, 'Revenue from our IT services businesses alone was $1 billion [£560 million]. During the year we made significant progress toward our goal of being the preferred provider of comprehensive solutions for our customers; our focus on innovation was a key enabler for this.' Wipro has the most mature Six Sigma programme in the industry and was the world's first IT services company to achieve P-CMM, CMMI and CMM Level 5 certification.

Visit www.wipro.com for more information.

Further information

- The **National Association of Software and Service Companies (NASSCOM)** is India's premier trade body and the chamber of commerce of the IT software and services industry in the country. It works closely with the government in formulating national IT policies and plays an active role in the international software community. See www.nasscom.org.

- The **Ministry of Communications and Information Technology's** vision is to make India an IT superpower by 2008, in order to create wealth, generate employment and stimulate IT-led economic growth. The department's functions cover IT policy, promotion of knowledge-based companies and ecommerce, promotion of IT education and IT-based training, the National Informatics Centre and the Electronics Export and Computer Software Promotion Council. The website provides access to information on the Indian industry. See www.mit.-gov.in.

- **Software Technology Parks of India (STPI)** have played a seminal role in establishing India as the premier offshore outsourcing location. Set-up by the Department of Communications and Information Technology in 1991, STPI's objectives are to encourage, promote and boost software exports from India. STPI maintains internal engineering resources to provide consulting, training and implementation services covering network design, system integration, installation, operations and maintenance of application networks and other facilities. See www.stpi.soft.net.

- **BPOIndia.org** provides information, advice, facts and figures about the business process outsourcing industry in India, how to set-up a facility in India, a description of government initiatives, relevant events and research reports. See www.bpoindia.org.
- Mark Kobayashi-Hillary (2004) *Outsourcing to India: The Offshore Advantage.* This excellent book aims to introduce India, the major players in the Indian service industry, the reasons why you should choose India as an offshore outsourcing destination and the steps you need to take to find and work with a local partner.
- Paul Davies (2004) *What's this India Business? Offshoring, Outsourcing and the Global Services Revolution.* Paul Davies is a former managing director of Unisys India. His book contains advice on outsourcing to India and how to conduct business in the country.

IRELAND

In the late 1990s the economy in Ireland boomed as a result of investment funds from the EU that helped regenerate the country's infrastructure. Some have described Ireland as leaping straight from an agricultural economy to a post-industrial one, as large IT companies moved in, bringing jobs and investment. However, economic growth has now slowed, unemployment is rising and the cost of living is high. GDP growth slowed to 2.5 per cent in 2003 against a background of weak global demand, reduced corporate profitability, much lower public spending and sharply contracting investment. A recovery is predicted in 2004, with economic growth once more accelerating to 4.2 per cent by 2005.

FACTS AND FIGURES

Full country name	Ireland
Capital city	Dublin
Population	3.9 million
Language	Official languages are English and Irish or Gaelic
Business environment index (10 maximum)	8.33

Information and communication technologies

Telephone mainlines	
Per 1,000 people	485
In largest city (per 1,000 people)	–
Cost of local call (per 3 minutes)	£0.08

Mobile phones (per 1,000 people)	729
International communications	
Cost of call to USA (per 3 minutes)	£0.86
ICT expenditures	
Total ICT	£3,653 million
ICT as % of GDP	6.2%
ICT business and government environment (ratings from 1 to 7; 7 is highest/best)	
Broadband internet access availability	3.9
Local specialized IT services availability	5.7
Competition in ISPs	3.8
Government online services availability	5.1
Laws relating to ICT use	4.8
Government prioritization of ICT	5.4

Offshore IT services industry

Although it cannot compete on price with low-cost countries such as India and China, Ireland does offer savings over other Western European countries and the USA and has developed an IT services industry that specializes in implementing and adapting packaged software applications for use in various European countries. The Irish government has actively supported the industry, offering foreign businesses grants on everything from capital investment to recruitment and training. Ireland's company tax rate is the lowest in Western Europe. Irish-owned software firms export around £858 million of software and services each year.

The software industry is concentrated primarily around Dublin; Galway and Cork are the other important centres. There are major universities at all three sites, which also have large business or technology parks. IT companies have introduced ISO and Six Sigma quality processes, but have not invested in CMM certification to the same extent as firms in India.

The only significant factor limiting further growth in the IT services sector is the relatively small population and hence limited pool of IT resources. About 5,000 technology students graduate each year and the multinational companies based in Ireland recruit many of these. This limits the expansion of indigenous Irish companies. Irish programmers are paid on average £14,000 to £23,000 annually, but Ireland's strong economy and early success as an offshore location are leading to increased costs.

Company profiles

Eontec

Eontec was founded in 1994 by banking and IT specialists who pioneered multi-channel banking solutions based on Java. Exclusively focused on the banking sector, the company's product comprises a suite of module-based solutions including branch, ebanking, call centre and multi-channel lending. Eontec can form a single solution or be implemented as part of an integrated suite. Clients include the Commonwealth Bank of Australia, Canadian Imperial Bank of Commerce and the Bank of Ireland. Eontec has offices in Europe, North America and Asia-Pacific. Eontec was acquired by Siebel Systems in April 2004.

Visit www.siebel.com for more information.

Prumerica Systems Ireland

Prumerica Systems Ireland is a fully owned subsidiary of Prudential Financial, one of the world's largest financial services organizations and employs over 380 people. Prumerica Systems Ireland encompasses two businesses based at Letterkenny, County Donegal. The first business, set up in 2000, is a software development subsidiary. Core activities are the development and maintenance of technology-based solutions to support the administration, marketing and sales of Individual Financial Services products. A wide range of technology is supported including mainframe, client/server, internet and integration between legacy and more modern systems. The second business has been operating since 2001, providing back-office contact centre services. The software development group has been compliant with CMM Level 3 for software product development and maintenance since 2003.

Visit www.prumerica.ie for more information.

Further information

- **IDA Ireland** is an Irish government agency with responsibility for securing new investment from overseas in manufacturing and internationally traded services sectors. It is funded by the Irish government under the National Development Plan, 2000–06. Over 1,050 overseas companies have chosen Ireland as their European base and are involved in a wide range of activities in sectors as diverse as ebusiness, engineering, information and communications technologies, pharmaceuticals, medical technologies, financial and international services. See www.ida.ie.

- The **Irish Software Association (ISA)**, which has represented the interests of software and computing services in Ireland since 1978, is the principal trade association for the software industry in Ireland. ISA's core mission is to promote the common interests of the software sector as a whole, as well as enabling members to exchange ideas, share resources, promote the industry and influence public policy. The association also helps software companies to start, manage and grow their firms and helps them to be successful in global markets. See www.software.ie.

ISRAEL

Israel is a bustling, noisy, modern country. As widely reported in the media, the threat of Palestinian suicide bombings and retaliatory strikes by Israeli Defence Forces mean that personal security in Israel is not reliable or predictable. The Lonely Planet website advises that travel to the region is not encouraged. The Prime Minister, Ariel Sharon, has put strains on his coalition with his pursuit of unilateral disengagement from the Palestinian Territories.

The slow recovery in the economy, in addition to spending cuts, will push the budget deficit down in 2004 (although it will remain high) falling to 3 per cent of GDP in 2005. The economy is likely to grow more robustly in 2005 as domestic demand improves.

FACTS AND FIGURES

Full country name	State of Israel
Capital city	Jerusalem
Population	6.5 million
Language	Official languages are Hebrew and Arabic; English is used extensively for government, commerce and educational purposes
Country risk score (100 = most risky)	37
Business environment index (10 maximum)	7.36

Information and communication technologies

Telephone mainlines	
Per 1,000 people	476
In largest city (per 1,000 people)	–
Cost of local call (per 3 minutes)	£0.01
Mobile phones (per 1,000 people)	808
International communications	
Cost of call to USA (per 3 minutes)	£1.85
ICT expenditures	
Total ICT	–
ICT as % of GDP	7.4%
ICT business and government environment (ratings from 1 to 7; 7 is highest/best)	
Broadband internet access availability	3.8
Local specialized IT services availability	–
Competition in ISPs	6.1
Government online services availability	3.9
Laws relating to ICT use	5.3
Government prioritization of ICT	5.8

Offshore IT services industry

With its highly skilled workforce, the Israeli software industry has concentrated on high-end niche software products and services. The industry develops products for the security, telecommunications, elearning, engineering and anti-virus software markets. Software products are exported to North America and Europe. Although the government has supported the industry through tax incentives and so on, equally important has been the emphasis on national security requirements and the major investment in high-tech security products. Many of the entrepreneurs who start Israeli IT companies developed their technical expertise working on defence-related security products.

Although Israel exports about £1.7 billion of software each year, the offshore services sector is relatively small, amounting to some £179 million annually. Political and security concerns would in any event deter many potential customers. In addition, the skilled Israeli workforce seeks out more complex and demanding work than the coding and maintenance work carried out in India or China. The software industry is based around Haifa, Tel Aviv and Jerusalem.

There are about 35,000 IT professionals in Israel, of which some 14,500 are employed as programmers in Israel's hundreds of software companies. An excellent education system and the government's emphasis on science and technology produce a highly skilled technical workforce. The labour force was boosted by the immigration of engineers and scientists from the former Soviet Union in the early 1990s.

Company profile

Intel

Intel set up its first design and development centre outside the USA in Haifa in 1974 and is now a leading exporter in the country. The Centrino mobile technology launched in 2003 was largely developed in Intel Israel's design centres. Intel has development centres at a number of locations including Jerusalem, Yakum and Omer, near Beer Sheba.

Visit www.intel.com/community for more information.

Further information

Founded in 1982, the **Israeli Association of Software Houses (IASH)** is the umbrella organization for Israeli software and IT companies and has over 100 members. IASH goals include the promotion of Israel as a world centre for software development and increased collaboration between Israel's software industry and potential partners around the world. 'Israel has emerged as a world centre for software research, development and production,' the Chairman of IASH, Amiram Shore wrote in 2001. 'Major multinational companies have established R&D centres in the country. These include IBM, Intel, Compaq, Hewlett Packard, Microsoft, Motorola,

National Semiconductor and others. Microsoft set up its first research centre outside of the US in Haifa, while Intel was so satisfied with its existing design facilities that it recently chose to open its largest R&D centre worldwide here in Israel. These investments have enabled the world's major players to explore new horizons and benefit from Israel's outstanding talent.' See www.iash.org.il.

MALAYSIA

Malaysia is a buoyant and wealthy South East Asian country, and has moved towards a pluralist culture based on a vibrant and interesting fusion of Malay, Chinese, Indian and indigenous cultures and customs. In the 2004 elections, the ruling Barisan Nasional coalition widened its majority in the federal parliament and thoroughly outperformed the opposition. Malaysia's economy is benefiting from the global recovery, but growth is due in part to public spending, which has been unsustainably high.

Malaysia is hot and humid all year. It is divided into two distinct parts: peninsular Malaysia and the eastern provinces of Sabah and Sarawak in North Borneo. More than 60 per cent of the country is still rainforest, but a government plan to build a huge hydroelectric dam in Sarawak is expected to decimate a huge area of forest. Malaysia is a multicultural society. The largest community, the Malays, are Muslims, speak Bahasa and are largely responsible for the political fortunes of the country. The Chinese are Buddhists and Taoists and account for about a third of the population. They are dominant in the business community and speak Hokkein, Hakka and Cantonese. About 10 per cent of the population are Indians, many of which are Hindu Tamils from southern India who speak Tamil, Malayalam and Hindi. When members of these different communities talk to each other they usually speak English, which has been reintroduced as the language of instruction in higher education.

FACTS AND FIGURES

Full country name	Federation of Malaysia
Capital city	Kuala Lumpur
Population	24.3 million
Language	Bahasa Malay is the official language; Chinese, English and Tamil are widely spoken
Country risk score (100 = most risky)	31
Business environment index (10 maximum)	7.02

Information and communication technologies

Telephone mainlines
- Per 1,000 people — 196
- In largest city (per 1,000 people) — 282
- Cost of local call (per 3 minutes) — £0.01

Mobile phones (per 1,000 people) — 314

International communications
- Cost of call to USA (per 3 minutes) — £1.33

ICT expenditures
- Total ICT — £3,542 million
- ICT as % of GDP — 6.6%

ICT business and government environment
(ratings from 1 to 7; 7 is highest/best)
- Broadband internet access availability — 3.4
- Local specialized IT services availability — 3.9
- Competition in ISPs — 4.4
- Government online services availability — 3.3
- Laws relating to ICT use — 4.8
- Government prioritization of ICT — 5.9

Offshore IT services industry

Prospects for Malaysia are improving with the government's £5.6 billion investment in two high-tech parks, Cyberjaya and Putrajaya, as part of its Multimedia Super Corridor project to attract international business. The core areas are equipped with high-capacity global telecommunications and logistics networks. Secure cyberlaws, strategic policies and a range of financial and non-financial incentives for investors also support the corridor. By 2011, local officials expect the high-tech corridor to be supporting a working population of around 50,000 and a resident population of more than 120,000. Today the corridor hosts more than 1,000 multinational, foreign-owned and Malaysian companies focused on multimedia and communications products, solutions and services as well as research and development. The corridor currently measures 15 by 50 kilometres. In future years the government plans to establish a web of similar corridors elsewhere in Malaysia, to pass a global framework of cyberlaws, to create more 'intelligent cities' and to set-up an International Cybercourt of Justice.

Malaysia offers a low wage structure but is constrained by a shortage of skilled IT workers. Many employees are recruited from India and China. The average annual programmer's salary is about £4,600 while an experienced software engineer can earn £17,000 a year. The government has established 'smart schools' that have the staff and equipment to train a larger IT workforce.

Company profile

HSBC

HSBC opened its sixth group service centre, HSBC Electronic Data Processing, in Cyberjaya in 2003. The centre handles selected global processing work such as credit analysis and trade services for countries such as New Zealand, Australia, Singapore, the UK, the USA, Canada and those in the Middle East. Over 500 employees work at the new centre, which is HSBC's first in South East Asia and larger than the service centres at Hyderabad, Bangalore, Shanghai and Guangzhou.

Visit www.hsbc.com for more information.

Further information

- **Cyberjaya**, the 'Intelligent City' combines a lush tropical eco-friendly environment with the latest infrastructure technology and facilities. The city spans 7,000 acres and combines enterprise, commercial and residential zones with public facilities and open space. See www.cyberjaya-msc.com.
- The **Multimedia Development Corporation** was established by the Malaysian government in 1996 to spearhead the development and implementation of the Multimedia Super Corridor. The corporation is dedicated to ensuring that the corridor is the world's best environment to harness the full potential of ICT and multimedia technology. See www.msc.com.my.
- The **Association of the Computer and Multimedia Industry, Malaysia (PIKOM)** is the trade association representing the ICT industry in Malaysia. Over 400 companies spanning a wide spectrum of ICT products and services are members, accounting for some 80 per cent of the total ICT trade in Malaysia. See www.pikom.org.my.

MEXICO

The oil boom of the late 1970s increased Mexico's oil revenues and financed industrial and agricultural investments, but the oil glut in the mid 1980s deflated petroleum prices and led to the worst recession in decades. The economic downturn also sparked an increase in political dissent. In the late 1980s and early 1990s, Mexico's crippling national debt was renegotiated, the rising inflation was brought under control and a wide-ranging privatization programme was launched.

The NAFTA trade alliance came into effect at the beginning of 1994. There were concerns that the alliance would harm the interests of the indigenous Mexicans and this led to uprisings and unrest that continues to this day. In March 1994, the Mexican currency suddenly collapsed, causing a deep economic recession. Among other things, this led to a huge increase in crime and a large-scale emigration to the USA.

Mexico has gradually pulled itself out of recession, despite the international economic slowdown in recent years. Rumours of government corruption are on the increase and a series of videos showing Mexican officials apparently engaged in corrupt practices is shaking up the political system and altering candidates' prospects for the 2006 presidential election.

FACTS AND FIGURES

Full country name	United Mexican States
Capital city	Mexico City
Population	100.9 million
Language	Spanish
Country risk score (100 = most risky)	42
Business environment index (10 maximum)	6.71

Information and communication technologies

Telephone mainlines	
Per 1,000 people	137
In largest city (per 1,000 people)	156
Cost of local call (per 3 minutes)	£0.09
Mobile phones (per 1,000 people)	217
International communications	
Cost of call to USA (per 3 minutes)	£1.70
ICT expenditures	
Total ICT	£10,758 million
ICT as % of GDP	3.2%
ICT business and government environment	
(ratings from 1 to 7; 7 is highest/best)	
Broadband internet access availability	4.2
Local specialized IT services availability	4.5
Competition in ISPs	3.7
Government online services availability	3.9
Laws relating to ICT use	3.3
Government prioritization of ICT	4.6

Offshore IT services industry

Mexico's strengths as an offshore location lie in its proximity to the USA, low wage levels and the NAFTA trade alliance, which allows the free flow of goods and services between Mexico, Canada and the USA and provides intellectual property rights in the three countries. Mexico also provides a useful entry point into other Latin American markets, which share the same language and similar culture.

The ICT sector is fragmented and most software services firms are very small. The outsource software services sector is only worth around £17 million annually. The offshore industry suffers from a lack of expertise and English language skills. Most Mexican programmers speak Spanish and, although firms are now investing in training, Mexico is still far behind India and the Philippines in English proficiency. There are only about 30,000 qualified programmers in Mexico with just a few thousand new graduates each year. At £2,900 per annum, average salary levels are low but there are not enough qualified professionals to meet requirements. The situation is made worse by the fact that many of those who graduate in Mexico prefer to move to the USA.

Recognizing the priority of the software industry, the Mexican government set-up the Programme for the Development of the Software Industry (PROSOFT), whose aims include market growth and an increase in ICT expenditure, which currently stands at only 3.2 per cent of GDP. The goal is for Mexico to become the leader in Latin America's software development and related services sector. The software industry is located around Mexico City and three technology parks in Monterrey and Guadalajara, which is Mexico's version of Silicon Valley.

Company profile

EDM International

EDM International, a General Electric company, has been providing outsourcing solutions for over 12 years in Mexico including imaging, document storage and retrieval services, mailroom operations and call centre services. The company has implemented Six Sigma techniques and has trained Master Black Belts on staff to supervise quality standards for all outsourced projects. With over 3,000 employees EDM is one of North America's largest offshore data capture firms. Clients include Federal Express, Airborne Express, Computer Sciences Corporation (CSC) and GE Capital.

Visit www.edmi.com for more information.

Further information

- Mexican Association of the Information Technology Industry (AMITI) www.amiti.org.mx (Spanish language only).

THE PHILIPPINES

The Philippines consists of over 7,000 islands in the western Pacific Ocean, only 2,000 of which are inhabited. About 6,000 of these islands are smaller than one square kilometre and 2,500 do not even have a name. This is an area of volcanic topography and the Philippines experience frequent seismic activity.

In 1998, a former film star, Joseph Estrada, was elected as president, probably based on his popular screen image. He promised economic wealth but was tried late in 2000 on charges of taking bribes from gambling syndicates. He resigned in January 2001 and was succeeded by his vice president, Gloria Arroyo, who promised to wipe out poverty and corruption. Arroyo found herself competing against another popular film star, Fernando Poe, in the 2004 presidential election. Although the validity of the result was not universally acknowledged, Arroyo was declared the winner with the backing of both houses of Congress. The government is expected to attempt to move ahead quickly with political and economic reforms.

The southern Philippines continues to be plagued by instability. The government signed a peace accord with the Moro National Liberation Front in 1996, granting considerable autonomy in many provinces. A splinter group, the militant Moro Islamic Liberation Front opposes the agreement, but long-delayed peace talks with the government may take place in 2004.

FACTS AND FIGURES

Full country name	Republic of the Philippines
Capital city	Manila
Population	79.9 million
Language	Filipino and English are the official languages. English is the language of government, commerce and media.
Country risk score (100 = most risky)	51
Business environment index (10 maximum)	6.39

Information and communication technologies

Telephone mainlines	
Per 1,000 people	42
In largest city (per 1,000 people)	265
Cost of local call (per 3 minutes)	–
Mobile phones (per 1,000 people)	150
International communications	
Cost of call to USA (per 3 minutes)	£2.69
ICT expenditures	
Total ICT	£1,753 million
ICT as % of GDP	4.2%

ICT business and government environment (ratings from 1 to 7; 7 is highest/best)	
Broadband internet access availability	3.6
Local specialized IT services availability	4.6
Competition in ISPs	4.4
Government online services availability	2.3
Laws relating to ICT use	4.1
Government prioritization of ICT	4.6

Offshore IT services industry

The Philippines is the third largest English-speaking country in the world and was a US protectorate for nearly 50 years. As an offshore location it therefore offers both excellent English language skills and knowledge of western culture. A large call centre and business process outsourcing industry has developed in the Philippines, though the IT services sector is more limited. The total outsourcing industry is worth £560 million annually and the offshore software services sector earns £196 million each year. The average IT salaries range from £2,800 to £5,600 per year.

The workforce in the Philippines is highly skilled – there are 86 universities producing 380,000 graduates each year, but there are not enough software programmers with only 10,000 new graduates from universities and IT training schools each year. This means that the Philippines does not have the resource pool to compete for large IT outsourcing contracts. There are currently about 30 offshore software service companies but none has achieved CMM certification. There have also been security and political concerns, though difficulties have been concentrated in the southern islands away from the offshore industry which is based around the capital in the area known as Metro Manila.

To foster more local IT companies, President Arroyo leads a taskforce that aims to stimulate the development of the Philippine IT industry and companies in the business process outsourcing sector. Companies that set up in the IT business parks benefit from a six-year tax holiday as well as exemptions from government fees, licenses and export taxes. The government has also formed the Information Technology and E-Commerce Council, an inter-agency government and private sector body that advises the government on IT and ecommerce policies and projects.

Company profiles

Software Ventures International

Software Ventures International (SVI) provides information management solutions to businesses in a wide range of industries including telecommunications, transportation, pharmaceuticals, chemical, publishing, media, banking, insurance, manufacturing, energy, retail, healthcare and government. Offshore contact centres form a major part of SVI's overall business. With the acquisition of US-based Telemarketing Concepts (TCI) in 2000, SVI has expanded its offerings to include in-bound customer support, human resources support and technical support call centre services, and out-bound telemarketing services provided by TCI. SVI has recently added business process outsourcing to its portfolio and now provides transcription services to the medical, legal and law enforcement industries.

Visit www.svi.com for more information.

Safeway

Safeway, one of North America's largest food and drug retailers, has set-up its own support and development centre in the Philippines. The centre is run by Safeway Philtec, a subsidiary of Safeway, and focuses on software development, maintenance and support. Safeway plans to consolidate all its US-based call centre operations and relocate these to the Philippines in 2004. According to Enrico Redona, IT group vice president and board director of Safeway Philtech, the company is committed to a long-term development and preferred partnership with the Philippines, 'Our commitment is based largely on our steadfast belief in Philippine talent and confidence in the reliability of its business environment.'

Visit www.safeway.com for more information (additional material from www.digitalphilippines.org).

Further information

- The **Digital Philippines Foundation** is a non-profit organization comprising ICT and ICT-related firms and associations, set-up to promote the development of the industry and the ICT profession. Founded in 2001, it was organized by the private sector members of the Information Technology and Electronic Commerce Council to channel private sector support for government IT initiatives. See www.digitalphilippines.org.
- **Outsource Philippines** is the one-stop information gateway to the country's key ICT activities of business process outsourcing, contact centres, medical and legal transcriptions, applications development and maintenance, animation, graphics, web development and computer-aided design. See www.outsourcephilippines.org.
- The **Information Technology Association of the Philippines (ITAP)** is a group of leading IT solutions providers in the country. It has represented the Philippine technological industry for over 20 years, offering business opportunities, executive networking, professional development programmes and other services. See www.itaphil.org.

POLAND

Located in the heartland of Europe, Poland has been both a bridge and a front line between Eastern and Western Europe. As communism gave way to democracy, Lech Walesa, leader of the Solidarity trade union became president in 1990, but was not able to deliver economic miracles or political stability. Poland is trying to raise itself off the ground and is gaining international credibility. It became a full NATO member in 1999 and joined the EU in 2004.

Although the current government led by Leszek Millar continues to be very unpopular, it looks set to serve its full term to 2005. Entry into the EU increases the importance of public sector reforms, but progress is constrained by domestic factors. The economy is recovering, with GDP growth expected to rise by 4.3 per cent in 2004 and 4.6 per cent in 2005.

With a strongly Roman Catholic population, Christian festivals are very important in Poland. Sculpture and painting are typically religious, with Gothic and Renaissance representations of the Madonna and Christ to be seen in most churches. Ornate tomb decoration was a particular speciality of Polish stone-workers. There are four daily meals in Poland; an early breakfast, a light snack for a second breakfast, a substantial lunch taken after work and a small supper before bed.

FACTS AND FIGURES

Full country name	Republic of Poland
Capital city	Warsaw
Population	38.6 million
Language	Polish; German and English are also spoken
Country risk score (100 = most risky)	37
Business environment index (10 maximum)	7.18

Information and communication technologies

Telephone mainlines	
Per 1,000 people	295
In largest city (per 1,000 people)	199
Cost of local call (per 3 minutes)	£0.04
Mobile phones (per 1,000 people)	260
International communications	
Cost of call to USA (per 3 minutes)	£1.64
ICT expenditures	
Total ICT	£5,874 million
ICT as % of GDP	5.9%

ICT business and government environment (ratings from 1 to 7; 7 is highest/best)	
Broadband internet access availability	4.0
Local specialized IT services availability	5.0
Competition in ISPs	3.5
Government online services availability	4.2
Laws relating to ICT use	4.1
Government prioritization of ICT	3.6

Offshore IT services industry

Poland has the largest working population of any country in Central Europe and one of the youngest with about 60 per cent under the age of 40. Some 35 per cent of the whole population are under the age of 25, and many young and well-educated people will be entering the labour market in future years. Since 2001, wages in Poland have been increasing very slowly due to high unemployment, and wage levels are now lower than in the Czech Republic and Hungary.

Graduates of Polish universities often speak more than one foreign language. Poland boasts nearly 100,000 scientists, of which less than 20 per cent currently work for the business sector. The country has 10 research centres (three times more than in the Czech Republic and Hungary).

Business process outsourcing companies in Poland include IBM (IT outsourcing), Thomson (accountancy) and Lufthansa (accountancy centre). Offshore service exports are worth roughly £45 million each year.

Company profile

American Management Systems

American Management Systems (AMS) is a business and IT consulting company, providing services to governments, financial services and communications industries around the globe. AMS specializes in enterprise resource planning, credit risk management, customer relationship management and enterprise security. Its headquarters are in Fairfax, Virginia and it has offices worldwide. AMS European headquarters are in The Hague, with staff and offices in 11 European countries. AMS has had a presence in Poland since 1996 with offices in Warsaw. It opened a development centre in Krakow in 2004 with 40 employees providing services to AMS projects around the world. Services include product maintenance and enhancements, application maintenance outsourcing, testing and systems re-engineering. 'AMS has an established and successful operation in Warsaw and we are confident we can replicate that success in Krakow,' Jonathan Bartlett, AMS engagement director for Poland said. 'The city is easily accessible, offers excellent business facilities and is already home to a number of software companies. Krakow provides us with access to a well-educated workforce with strong technical and functional skills.' AMS was acquired by CGI in May 2004.

Visit www.ams.com and www.cgi.com for more information.

Further information

- The **Polish Information and Foreign Investment Agency** was established in 2003 to coordinate the economic promotion of Poland, stimulate the inflow of foreign direct investment, assist foreign companies looking to invest in Poland and promote Polish exports. See www.paiz.gov.pl.
- The **Polish Chamber of Information Technology and Telecommunications (PIIT)** was founded in 1993 and now has over 170 members from the IT and telecommunications sector. PIIT has explained and helped improve legislation, tax, customs and copyright regulation as well as public tender procedures. It also promotes the Polish IT market and IT companies, supporting the 'Komputer Expo Fair' in Warsaw and 'Internet' in Kielce. See www.piit.org.pl.

ROMANIA

Romania lies on the Black Sea and the forested Carpathian Mountains account for one-third of the country's area, with another third covered by hills, orchards and vineyards, and the final part consisting of a fertile plain where cereals, vegetables and herbs are grown. The notorious prime minister, Nicolae Ceausescu (1965–89) was a skilled foreign policy operator who condemned Soviet intervention in Czechoslovakia in 1968, earning himself praise and economic aid from the West. On the domestic front, however, he was self-centred and inept. His grand projects were mostly expensive failures. His secret police kept a tight grip on society, recruiting a vast network of informers. In the late 1980s, Ceausescu decided to export Romania's food to pay off the country's mounting debt. While he and his wife lived in luxury, Romanian people struggled to feed themselves. Protest riots broke out and, late in 1989, the Ceausescus tried to flee Romania, but they were arrested, tried by an anonymous court and executed on Christmas Day.

The 1990s saw power shift from one political party to another, against a backdrop of rampant inflation, unemployment and allegations of government corruption. One of the most sensitive issues was the status of the country's sizeable Hungarian minority population. The current ruling Social Democratic Party has the difficult task of having to please the EU and the IMF as well as the Romanian people at the same time. Their declining popularity makes the outcome of the parliamentary election late in 2004 difficult to predict. The economy is forecast to grow by 5.0 per cent in 2004 and 5.2 per cent in 2005, driven by the rapid expansion of investment.

FACTS AND FIGURES

Full country name	Romania
Capital city	Bucharest
Population	21.8 million
Language	Romanian is the official language; Hungarian and German are widely understood
Country risk score (100 = most risky)	46
Business environment index (10 maximum)	6.03

Information and communication technologies

Telephone mainlines	
Per 1,000 people	184
In largest city (per 1,000 people)	368
Cost of local call (per 3 minutes)	£0.06
Mobile phones (per 1,000 people)	172
International communications	
Cost of call to USA (per 3 minutes)	£1.10
ICT expenditures	
Total ICT	£535 million
ICT as % of GDP	2.2%
ICT business and government environment (ratings from 1 to 7; 7 is highest/best)	
Broadband internet access availability	4.4
Local specialized IT services availability	2.9
Competition in ISPs	3.4
Government online services availability	1.2
Laws relating to ICT use	3.1
Government prioritization of ICT	4.0

Offshore IT services industry

Romania offers a skilled labour force, which is well trained in engineering and technology, and available at competitive wage rates. The majority of Romania's engineers graduate from technical institutes in Bucharest, Chij, Iasi and Timisoara and the ICT industry has developed around these centres of excellence. There are about 5,000 companies in the software and IT services market and exports are growing at approximately 35 per cent each year. Each year about 5,000 new computer specialist graduates join the workforce. The cost of employing a recently qualified graduate from an approved specialist university is about £3,700 a year, with an experienced project manager earning between £12,000 and £18,000 a year. In 2003, revenue for offshore IT services from European countries reached about £70 million, mostly from France, Germany, the UK and the Netherlands (www.zdnn.com).

Company profiles

IPACRI

IPACRI is a top-ten Romanian outsourcing software exporter that achieved certification of compliance with ISO 9001:2001 in 2004 and is working towards compliance with CMM Level 3. Established in 1994, IPACRI employs more than 50 highly skilled programmers and provides software development and IT consultancy in banking and finance, postal services, sales force automation and knowledge management. Its clients are based in the Middle East, throughout Europe and in the USA. IPACRI's major shareholder is the ELSAG Group from Italy.

Visit www.ipacri.ro for more information.

ARoBS Transilvania Software

ARoBS Transilvania Software specializes in offshore software development for countries in Europe and North America. Expertise in C++, Java and AS/400 is offered. The company was founded in 1998 by a group of young engineers with experience working for companies in Germany and the USA.

Visit www.arobs.com for more information.

ADCOS

ADCOS is a software company established in 1996 in Romania with German capital, specializing in enterprise resource planning solutions. ADCOS provides offshore outsourcing software and web development services.

Visit www.adcos.ro for more information.

Further information

- The ROMANIAN ASSOCIATION FOR THE ELECTRONIC AND SOFTWARE INDUSTRY (ARIES) aims to promote and protect the Romanian IT and electronic business environment, as well as the professional and commercial interests of its members. ARIES has more than 280 members and is the largest ICT association in Romania. It has developed strategies on Romanian high-tech potential and turning Romania into an important global software producer and exporter. See www.aries.ro.

- The NATIONAL ASSOCIATION OF THE SOFTWARE INDUSTRY AND SERVICES (ANIS) was established as a non-profit organization in 1998. It currently has about 80 members and aims to promote the ICT industry in Romania by stimulating demand, improving quality, seeking to influence government and the media both in Romania and abroad, organizing conferences and exhibitions and supporting education and training. See www.anis.ro.

- ROMANIAN ASSOCIATION FOR INFORMATION TECHNOLOGY AND COMMUNICATIONS (ATIC), www.atic.org.ro (Romanian language only).

RUSSIA

Despite the demise of the USSR, Russia is still huge. From its borders in the west it stretches 6,000 kilometres to the Pacific Ocean in the east. The landscape is predominantly flat, punctuated only by the Urals and the mountain ranges of Siberia in the far east. Russia's cultural achievements from the 19th century in literature, architecture, ballet, musical composition and performance are outstanding. The most characteristic architectural feature is the onion-domed church, which evolved when the wooden churches of the north were translated into brick and colourful tile work. Russian is the language of state business and the native tongue of over half the population. The people in Central Asia speak Turk.

Moves towards a deregulated market economy in Russia have been accompanied by stories of rampant crime and prostitution, relentless drug-trafficking and long queues for non-existent food. Vladimir Putin became president in 2000 and his authoritarian style has made him popular but raised concerns about modernization policies in Russia. Putin is likely to push ahead with economic reforms and fiscal policy will be prudent.

FACTS AND FIGURES

Full country name	Russian Federation
Capital city	Moscow
Population	144 million
Language	Russian; each ethnic minority also has its own language
Country risk score (100 = most risky)	45
Business environment index (10 maximum)	5.85

Information and communication technologies

Telephone mainlines	
Per 1,000 people	243
In largest city (per 1,000 people)	463
Cost of local call (per 3 minutes)	£0.01
Mobile phones (per 1,000 people)	38
International communications	
Cost of call to USA (per 3 minutes)	£3.43

ICT expenditures	
Total ICT	£5,548 million
ICT as % of GDP	3.3%
ICT business and government environment	
(ratings from 1 to 7; 7 is highest/best)	
Broadband internet access availability	2.7
Local specialized IT services availability	4.4
Competition in ISPs	3.6
Government online services availability	2.6
Laws relating to ICT use	3.0
Government prioritization of ICT	3.7

Offshore IT services industry

Russia has tremendous potential as an offshore location. It has an ample supply of scientific and engineering expertise. Each year, over 25,000 physics, mathematics, informatics and computer engineering students graduate. Average IT salaries range from £3,500 to £6,000. There are a large number of local software companies, most of which have been set up since 1993. Many of these firms hope to enter outsourcing deals with western companies. The Russian software export market earned £266 million in 2003, a 60 per cent increase over 2002.

There are, however, a number of constraints that detract from Russia's ability to compete in global markets. The unstable economy, lack of management expertise and poor protection for data and intellectual property cause problems. The lack of effective government support is a significant factor. Russia is still hindered by a complex bureaucracy, restrictive laws and endless taxes. Although the Russian government recognizes the importance of the IT industry, it is moving very slowly towards the tax incentives and business friendly environment introduced in other countries to stimulate the IT industry. The situation is hampered by a lack of clear responsibility within government for the ICT sector. Three different ministries (the Economic Development and Trade Ministry; the Industry, Science and Technology Ministry; and the Telecommunications and Information Ministry) are all involved but do not cooperate effectively. In 2001 the government launched the 'Electronic Russia' programme aimed at developing the ICT sector and this was well received by the Russian IT industry, although there has been little progress.

Most of Russia's offshore IT services companies are based in Moscow, St. Petersburg, Yekaterinburg and Novosibirsk in Siberia. Each of these cities is home to a major university that is well known for the high standard of education. Infrastructure is generally poor and bandwidth costs are high except in the technology parks. Russia's own software services companies tend to be small; the average firm has about 110 employees. The ISO quality standards are widely adopted, but Russia has only a limited number of CMM certified companies. Much of the offshore work carried out in Russia takes place in development centres set-up for USA and European companies to help build markets and to use the talent of Russian programmers for high-end development work.

Company profiles

EPAM

EPAM, the largest provider of software outsourcing services and ecommerce solutions in Central and Eastern Europe, provides software development, ecommerce and content services to companies and government organizations in over 30 countries worldwide. Founded in 1993, EPAM has its North American headquarters in Princeton, New Jersey and its European headquarters in Budapest. EPAM's offshore development centres are in Moscow, Budapest and Minsk, Belarus. There are also account management and sales resources in Minneapolis, Minnesota and London. Most system development work is carried out in EPAM's state-of-the-art development facilities in Moscow, Budapest and Minsk. EPAM's methodology is to use a local, onsite resource of at least one EPAM consultant to develop the business requirements and to manage the project, combined with world-class offshore software development teams. Software engineering processes in EPAM are certified to ISO 9001:2000 and in September 2003 the Minsk Development Centre became the first software organization in Europe to pass a formal assessment at CMMI Level 4. EPAM's customers include Reuters, Colgate-Palmolive, Halliburton, Samsung America and Bally of Switzerland.

Visit www.epam.com for more information.

LUXOFT

LUXOFT is a member of the IBS Group, Russia's largest IT company and has over 700 employees and development centres in Moscow, St Petersburg, Dubna and Omsk. LUXOFT's customers include Boeing, IBM, Dell and Citibank. It was the first company in the world to achieve CMM and CMMI Level 5 certifications simultaneously, as well as the first company in Europe to achieve CMMI Level 5. In March 2004, LUXOFT opened an office in London to support operations in the UK and the EU. Another office in Frankfurt is planned for 2004 as LUXOFT looks to increase its business with European companies.

Visit www.luxoft.com for more information.

Further information

- **Outsourcing-Russia.com** is a non-profit dedicated portal serving the interests of Russia's offshore software development companies and of international customers seeking information about the IT resources available within the Russian Federation. The portal was founded by

Star Software, a leading Russian software vendor (www.star-sw.com). Other participating companies include Beiten Burkhardt, an international Germany-based law firm with offices in Moscow and St. Petersburg. See www.outsourcing-russia.com.

- The **National Software Development Association of Russia (RUS-SOFT)** represents more than 50 companies from Russia and Belarus, employing some 5,000 highly qualified software developers. See www.russoft.org. In May 2004 RUSSOFT merged with the Fort Ross Information Technology Services Consortium (see www.forst-ross.ru for more information).

- Leading Russian companies formed the **National Software Development Alliance 'Silicon Taiga'** to promote the development of the IT outsourcing and software development industry. The Alliance serves the interests of its members and the offshore programming industry as a whole. See www.nsda.net.

- **Information and Computer Technologies Industry Association (APKIT)** www.apkit.ru (Russian language only).

SINGAPORE

Singapore is the food capital of Asia, with Chinese, Indian, Malay, Indonesian and western foods on offer. Street performances are held during important festivals such as the Chinese New Year. The Lion Dance is a spectacular, acrobatic dance usually performed during Chinese festivals. Older Singaporeans are keen on Chinese opera, an ancient form of theatre with highly stylized acting. Singapore consists of the main, low-lying Singapore island and 63 smaller islands.

Singapore developed as a flourishing colony with a military and naval base in the 19th century. Lee Kuan Yew, leader of the People's Action Party was prime minister from 1959 until 1990 and Singapore became the economic success story of the region. A shrewd operator, Lee established a strict social order and suppressed political opposition. In the late 1990s, Singapore suffered from the economic downturn that spread across South East Asia, but it is now on the road to recovery. GDP growth is expected to accelerate from 1.1 per cent in 2003 to 5.3 per cent annually in 2004–05, in line with a recovery in the global economy and in domestic business and consumer sentiment.

FACTS AND FIGURES

Full country name	Republic of Singapore
Capital city	Singapore
Population	4.2 million
Language	English, Chinese, Tamil and Malay

Country risk score (100 = most risky)	16
Business environment index (10 maximum)	8.53

Information and communication technologies

Telephone mainlines	
Per 1,000 people	471
In largest city (per 1,000 people)	471
Cost of local call (per 3 minutes)	£0.01
Mobile phones (per 1,000 people)	724
International communications	
Cost of call to USA (per 3 minutes)	£0.38
ICT expenditures	
Total ICT	£5,372 million
ICT as % of GDP	9.9%
ICT business and government environment	
(ratings from 1 to 7; 7 is highest/best)	
Broadband internet access availability	5.8
Local specialized IT services availability	5.2
Competition in ISPs	5.3
Government online services availability	6.4
Laws relating to ICT use	5.4
Government prioritization of ICT	6.2

Offshore IT services industry

The small island of Singapore is regarded as one of the most wired countries in the world. It has a highly skilled workforce of 2 million people. Many global firms such as IBM and EDS choose Singapore for their Asia headquarters, but compared to other Asian locations Singapore is expensive. The average annual programmer salary is about £11,200. The core competences offered by the offshore software services industry are application development and maintenance and system integration services.

The government aims to establish Singapore as South East Asia's financial and high-tech hub, with a goal of 6 million IT workers. Many workers come from outside the country at present and Singapore companies are outsourcing their work to India and China. Over the next few years the government aims to complete its Singapore ONE project leading to connectivity for every home, school and business (including government offices).

The Technology Corridor, in the south-west of Singapore, is an area of high concentration of knowledge-based industries, research and development organizations and universities. The intention is that networking between the researchers at the different organizations will result in collaborative projects. The Singapore Science Park is located at the heart of the Technology Corridor. Research and tertiary institutions such as the Kent Ridge Digital Labs, the Institute of High Performance Computing, the Institute of Microelectronics and the Centre for Wireless Communications, as well as national agencies such as the National Science and Technology Board are close to, or based within, the Science Park.

Company profile

NCS

NCS (formerly known as National Computer Systems) was initially established as a wholly owned subsidiary of Singapore's National Computer Board. It was privatized in 1991 and is now a subsidiary of the SingTel Group, with offices in Australia, China, Malaysia, India and elsewhere. NCS offers a wide range of services including consulting, application development, system integration, IT infrastructure and out-sourcing services. Its customers span the Asia Pacific region and include Brunei Telecom, Singapore Airlines, Citibank Asia Pacific Technology Group and the Shanghai National Accounting Institute. The company reached CMM Level 3 in November 2003.

Visit www.ce.ncs.com.sg for more information.

Further information

- The **Singapore infocomm Technology Federation (SiTF)** is Singapore's leading ICT trade industry association and has 600 corporate members from both multinational and local companies, which together account for over 80 per cent of the industry's revenues. SiTF assists business development, provides market intelligence and supports overseas trade missions, networking and alliances. It also organizes a number of events including the annual enterprise computing conference, iX200x, and 'Made in Singapore and Proud of IT!' See www.sitf.org.sg.

- The **Singapore Science Park** is home to over 300 companies, of which some 40 per cent are IT firms. Tenants include Sony, Lucent Technologies, Seagate Technology International, FujiXerox and Motorola Electronics. The Science Park was set-up under a government initiative in 1980 to provide new infrastructure needed to support research and development in Singapore. It was privatized in 1990 and is now owned by Ascendas. The Science Park is located in Singapore's Technology Corridor, and is set amidst lush, beautifully landscaped grounds in close proximity to the central business district and the Jurong industrial estate. See www.sciencepark.com.sg.

SOUTH AFRICA

South Africa continues to go through huge upheavals as it comes to terms with democracy. The changes have been both good and bad – from the dismantling of apartheid to the well-publicized crime problem. The African National Congress (ANC) came to power as a result of the free elections in 1994 with Nelson Mandela as president. Thabo Mbeki took over the leadership and became president in the 1999 elections. He has been generally effective, but his reputation is somewhat tarnished by his ill-informed comments on AIDS.

Despite the scars of the past, South Africa today is more relaxed and optimistic. Economic inequality remains a serious problem and it will be some time before the black majority experience economic benefits for themselves. The AIDS health crisis has affected 4.2 million South Africans and threatens to overwhelm all other domestic concerns. But South Africa is rediscovering itself with gallery retrospectives featuring contemporary and traditional black artists, and musicians from around Africa performing in major festivals. South Africa's wildlife wins the prizes – it has the largest mammal (the African elephant), the smallest mammal (the pigmy shrew), the tallest mammal (the giraffe), the fastest mammal (the cheetah), the largest bird (the ostrich) and the largest flying bird (the Kori bustard).

FACTS AND FIGURES

Full country name	Republic of South Africa
Capital city	Pretoria
Population	43.6 million
Language	Official languages are Afrikaans, English, Zulu, Xhosa, Swazi, Ndebele, Venda, Tsonga, Northern Sotho, Western Sotho, and Southern Sotho
Country risk score (100 = most risky)	45
Business environment index (10 maximum)	6.31

Information and communication technologies

Telephone mainlines	
Per 1,000 people	112
In largest city (per 1,000 people)	415
Cost of local call (per 3 minutes)	£0.04
Mobile phones (per 1,000 people)	252

International communications
    Cost of call to USA (per 3 minutes)   £0.32
ICT expenditures
    Total ICT   £6,401 million
    ICT as % of GDP   9.2%
ICT business and government environment
(ratings from 1 to 7; 7 is highest/best)
    Broadband internet access availability   3.7
    Local specialized IT services availability   5.4
    Competition in ISPs   4.3
    Government online services availability   3.6
    Laws relating to ICT use   4.0
    Government prioritization of ICT   4.5

Offshore IT services industry

Thanks to a rich diversity of cultures and languages, South Africa offers a well-educated workforce with a high level of diction and dialect proficiency not only in English but also in many European languages such as French, German, Italian, Portuguese, Dutch and Flemish. Wage rates are competitive, if not the cheapest in the world, and average programmer rates are in the region of £5,000 to £9,100 per year. Due at least in part to high unemployment levels, attrition rates are low – a particularly attractive benefit to call centre operations, which often suffer from high staff turnover rates.

South Africa has a well-developed financial services infrastructure, an open and transparent business environment and an affinity to European culture. The UK is the largest foreign investor in the country and there are strong business ties between the two nations. The liberalization of the telecommunications industry is leading to significant infrastructure developments, and services at least in urban areas are of a high standard and reliable. Power supplies are also robust and cost-effective.

As well as a strong work ethic, South Africans are known for lateral thinking and the development of ideas and concepts. The high cost of imported systems that often need to be adapted for local use has encouraged the domestic market to find innovative and cost-effective solutions. The country's advances in security software and in the banking sector illustrate South African creative thinking.

The government supports industry development and offers a range of incentives to foreign investors. The South African Department of Trade and Industry has played an active role in the development of the information and communication technology and electronics sectors through the establishment of the ICT Development Council. Chaired by the Minister of Trade and Industry, the Council represents all sectors of the industry and includes multinational companies as well as large, medium-sized and small local firms.

Company profiles

Computer Sciences Corporation

Computer Sciences Corporation (CSC) set-up a business process outsourcing operation in South Africa in 2003 to attract offshore work, with facilities in Cape Town and Johannesburg. CSC South Africa provides offshore SAP application support services to Anglian Water, the UK utility, with the majority of the support work delivered from South Africa. A team of staff on the helpdesk in the UK log customer problems, queries and requests in a queue. The calls are transferred to the South African team, who in effect become an extension of the UK support centre. 'CSC's high volume, low complexity work now goes to India and the more complex but lower volume work comes to SA,' according to Peter Drube, business process outsourcing director at CSC South Africa. 'By doing this, we spread risk and can start balancing the work load.' CSC opened its South Africa facilities to complement its Indian operations. Factors taken into account were South Africa's exchange rate, the country's political risk, the state of the financial sector and general infrastructure such as telecommunications. CSC already employs over 120 people in South Africa and expects to employ more than 1,000 by 2009.

Visit www.csc.com for more information (additional material from free.financialmail.co.za).

Dialogue Group

The UK-based Dialogue Group bought into a Cape Town call centre business with 110 employees in 2003. By the end of 2004 the Dialogue Group Cape Town office expects to employ nearly 1,000 people. Clients include Adcock Ingram, British American Tobacco, E-media, Fox Group and Pfizer Pharmaceuticals. A new office in Johannesburg will be opened in 2004. 'It's a combination of people with a can-do attitude, who are gracious, professional and interested in their work because they've been properly trained, and South Africa's competitive pricing and highly developed infrastructure that brings us the business,' according to Mark Spendlove, International Marketing Director. Dialogue has also invested in Absolutvalu, possibly the only black call centre in the country, which is involved in training historically disadvantaged Afrikaans speakers to speak Dutch to handle business in Holland.

Visit www.dialogue-group.com for more information.

Further information

- **SAVANT** is a public–private partnership between government and industry. It is the vanguard of the South African information and communication technology and electronics sectors. Supported by leading industry partners and the ICT Development Council, SAVANT's role is to promote South African innovation both locally and abroad. The goal of SAVANT is to establish a foundation awareness campaign by marketing the industry domestically. It also aims to strengthen the sector in order to add dimension to its global competitiveness. See www.savant.co.za.

- **Information Industry South Africa** is an association of associations, facilitating communication between stakeholders in the South African information and communication technology and electronics industries, and promoting the growth of the sector and the development of technical skills. The organization progresses its goals by engaging with government departments, issuing position papers on matters of national importance, organizing premier exhibitions and conferences such as Futurex and representing the industry in world forums. See www.informationindustry.org.za.

VIETNAM

Vietnam is made up of equatorial lowlands, high-temperate plateaus and cooler mountainous areas. It has a diverse wildlife that is in rapid decline due to the destruction of habitats, illegal hunting and pollution. Although it has few visitors, Vietnam has 10 national parks and an expanding range of nature reserves. Vietnamese cuisine is very varied – there are said to be nearly 500 different traditional dishes that include exotic meats and fantastic vegetarian creations.

There seems little risk to the Communist Party's continued political supremacy. The deputies in the National Assembly are increasingly assertive, so the Party's leaders may have some difficulties in pushing through their agenda unchallenged, but there appears to be little prospect of meaningful political opposition in the next few years. The current leadership will support economic reform and GDP growth is likely to remain strong in 2004–05, driven by an expanding private sector.

FACTS AND FIGURES

Full country name	Socialist Republic of Vietnam
Capital city	Hanoi
Population	80.5 million
Language	Vietnamese or Quoc-Ngu is the official language; French, Chinese, English, Khmer and various tribal languages are also spoken

Country risk score (100 = most risky)	52
Business environment index (10 maximum)	5.17

Information and communication technologies

Telephone mainlines	
Per 1,000 people	38
In largest city (per 1,000 people)	133
Cost of local call (per 3 minutes)	£0.01
Mobile phones (per 1,000 people)	15
International communications	
Cost of call to USA (per 3 minutes)	–
ICT expenditures	
Total ICT	£1,189 million
ICT as % of GDP	6.7%
ICT business and government environment (ratings from 1 to 7; 7 is highest/best)	
Broadband internet access availability	2.7
Local specialized IT services availability	3.4
Competition in ISPs	2.7
Government online services availability	2.2
Laws relating to ICT use	2.8
Government prioritization of ICT	4.7

Offshore IT services industry

Vietnam offers a well-educated workforce and low wage costs. Graduates usually lack adequate English proficiency, particularly in spoken English. Programmers earn around £2,000 to £3,400 annually, but managers requiring more experience and better English skills may be paid 20 per cent more. Telecommunications, power and buildings all need improvement and there is still uncertainty about the region's stability.

By 2005, the Vietnamese government wants to employ 50,000 IT workers and become part of the World Trade Organization. There is a lot to be done – the banking system, infrastructure and phone system all need to be modernized. Saigon Software Park is Vietnam's first advanced software development area with high-speed internet access and virtual private network capabilities.

Company profiles

Global CyberSoft

Global CyberSoft has its headquarters in Silicon Valley and operates one of the largest private software outsourcing operations in Vietnam. In California, Global CyberSoft has a team of experienced software project managers and engineers who provide quotations and project management backed up by the cost-competitive software team in HoChiMinh City. The company has in-depth experience in semiconductor factory automation and business automation, and offers a broad range of IT consulting and outsourcing services tailored to customers' needs. The offshore development centre is the largest facility inside Saigon Software Park and is ISO 9001 certified.

Visit www.globalcybersoft.com for more information.

Harvey Nash

Harvey Nash is a leading provider of IT recruitment and offshore development solutions with an annual turnover of more than £150 million. The company's development facility in Vietnam employs over 450 skilled architects, analysts, software designers and developers. The main focus is on software development using web and middleware technologies and all programmers have extensive object-orientation skills. Dedicated offshore development teams have been established for some customers. The offshore facility is certified to ISO 9001 and CMM Level 5. Harvey Nash also has full time staff in Europe and combines onshore and offshore working to minimize risk and improve communication with customers.

Visit www.harveynash-vn.com for more information.

Further information

- **Vietnam Software Association (VINASA)** www.vinasa.org (Vietnamese language only).

6 The Future World of Global Sourcing

Today global outsourcing is a £308 billion industry. India's success in the market is encouraging many other countries to develop their own offshore industry and each, as we have seen, has its own strengths and weaknesses and is finding its niche in the global marketplace. The global IT services industry looks set to continue its rapid growth. But today the top five players do not even have 20 per cent market share and we are likely to see many mergers and acquisitions over coming years. (www.computerworld.com). Competition for business is increasing and the current relatively high profit margins are unlikely to be sustainable over time. As prices increase or currency strengthens in one part of the world, other countries will become more cost competitive. Speaking at the CEO Conclave of the NASSCOM 2004 India Leadership Forum, the chief executive of Xansa, Alistair Cox said:

> **Corporate globality is about building relationships to bridge distance. It is about optimizing activities as if the world is a single marketplace. It is about developing a focused strategy based on economic logic and analysis then translating the strategy into local action.**
>
> www.xansa.com

Today offshore sourcing is commonly associated with routine work, whether that be low level program coding or call centre enquiries. But we can already see the beginnings of a higher value offshore industry developing. Author and consultant Mark Kobayashi-Hillary told me:

> **Services will certainly increase in value. I am now talking to architects who have associates working on draft diagrams offshore, accountants working with offshore UK and US tax experts and lawyers who are sourcing remote paralegal services. These services are already far beyond the scripted call centres of just a few years back, and the complexity will only increase.**
>
> **Investment banks are now seeking PhD and MBA holders in remote countries to work on their equity research and this entire change in the global service industry means that companies and employees need to rethink the world of work. Individuals can no longer think of work and employment conforming to national boundaries as companies will increasingly seek the best people in the best location, regardless of where their physical headquarters may be.**

Perhaps the worst thing we could do is pretend that globalization in the IT services market is not happening. We will achieve much more by building on the possibilities that it opens up. As Mark Kobayashi-Hillary wrote in *The Observer* (4 April 2004):

> **The logical conclusion to the global connectivity offered by the internet and almost-free voice calls is that any task not requiring a physical presence can be performed in the cheapest – or best – location for any particular domain. Society is witnessing the death of distance every day. This sense of global change may frighten some observers, but it is a thrilling time to be a manager.**
>
> **observer.guardian.co.uk/business**

Dramatic newspaper headlines and exaggerated claims about job losses make it difficult to have a balanced public debate about the impact of global sourcing. Maryfran Johnson, editor in chief of *Computerworld*, wrote:

> **Candid, open discussion about offshore outsourcing is the new corporate taboo. Nothing will be more politically incorrect this year than expressing interest in offshoring. What is often overlooked in the emotional, angry reactions to offshore outsourcing is how small a percentage it really occupies in the huge global outsourcing market.**
>
> **www.computerworld.com**

We surely need to share lessons learnt and develop best practices if we are to fully exploit the opportunities that global sourcing gives us.

How should IT professionals adapt to the world of global sourcing? According to John Mahoney, managing vice president, IT business management research at Gartner:

> **As the rising trend of outsourcing continues, internal IT roles will increasingly concentrate on core business value while managing and integrating external partners. In the longer term, all businesses will have to confront fundamental changes being created by the forces of globalisation, enterprise virtualization, increased focus on external relationships, economic cycles, increased regulatory control and their underlying technology enablers.**
>
> **www.computing.co.uk**

Speaking at the Gartner 2004 Spring Symposium, chief executive Michael Fleisher said,

> **IT must help the company understand what, and what not, to outsource – and show how it can be done. We are uniquely placed to take charge.**
>
> **www.computing.co.uk**

Discussion about offshore sourcing all too often focuses on the negative, but increasing globalization opens up opportunities for IT professionals both to work overseas and to provide services from the UK to worldwide markets. According to a comment column in *Computing*:

> As an industry that has been the cause of so much change in the past 30 years, it seems a little churlish to say that fear of change could be holding us back today. Concern over jobs moving offshore hinders progress on becoming part of a globalised industry that will create more higher-level, better paid jobs. More than ever, the IT community needs to talk in terms of people, not last-century press release buzzwords that reinforce the image of technology as scary and complex. IT leaders need to embrace change and demonstrate the inclusiveness of technology to colleagues and customers to ease their fears, and so take a controlling role in realizing the benefits of IT and the growth that will follow as a result.
>
> www.computing.co.uk

Since the very early days of computing, technology has opened up new opportunities and changed working lives. Predicting the future is almost impossible. The one thing we can be certain about is change and the challenge for those of us working as IT professionals is to exploit the benefits that each new development brings.

Appendix: Intellect Offshore Group Code of Practice

Intellect Offshore Group Members agree to conform to the following Code of Practice. Offshore Group Members agree to make this document available to all customers or partners in the UK.

1. SALES PROTOCOL

To ensure a professional sales approach to client prospecting by members. Respect the privacy of prospects' 'personal' contact details, e.g. direct lines, mobile telephone numbers, and not use these for unsolicited sales calls. Utilize a fax preference service before sending unsolicited faxes. Will not send random, untargeted commercial email. Include a mechanism for the recipient to register an objection to receiving future unsolicited e-mails.

2. REPRESENTATIONS

Will represent your company's true capabilities and organizational strength in a clear and concise manner:

(a) Resumes

Biographical details of candidates, supplied in any form, will be true to the best knowledge of the supplier, who will have previously taken all such steps as may be reasonably required to satisfy themselves of the accuracy of the detail.

(b) Human resources

Will provide the correct information regarding the number of staff and their experience and qualification.

(c) Infrastructure

Will provide complete and correct information regarding their infrastructure: such as office facilities and locations, hardware, software, ICT connectivity. Will clearly indicate their partnerships and relationships with other organizations.

(d) Client references

Client references should accurately state the member companies' involvement in any projects.

3. QUALITY POLICY

Will provide access to written confirmation of their Quality Policy, including relevant documentation including certification of any quality accreditation body.

4. IMMIGRATION

Always respect the Immigration rules, regulations and procedures of the countries in which they are conducting business.

5. RELATIONSHIP MANAGEMENT

Manage relationships in a proactive manner to ensure customer satisfaction. Take prompt action to rectify errors. Provide clear contact points and escalation processes for the resolution of disputes.

6. PROTECTION OF IPR/CONFIDENTIALITY

(a) Ownership of IPR

Will ensure that ownership of IPR is made clear within the contract and adhere to any such restrictions implied by this.

(b) Confidentiality

Will respect client confidentiality and ensure that their employees adhere to this as well.

To the customer:

Should you be unhappy with the performance of any of the member companies of the Intellect Offshore Group in respect of this Code of Practice, then please contact Intellect.

Source: www.intellectuk.org/groups

References

Cullen, S. and Willcocks, L. P. (2003) *Intelligent IT Outsourcing: Eight Building Blocks to Success.* Butterworth-Heinemann, Oxford.

Davies, P. (2004) *What's this India Business? Offshoring, Outsourcing and the Global Services Revolution.* Nicholas Brealey, London.

Galin, D. (2004) *Software Quality Assurance: From Theory to Implementation.* Pearson Education, Harlow.

Kobayashi-Hillary, M. (2004) *Outsourcing to India: The Offshore Advantage.* Springer-Verlag, Berlin.

McKinsey Global Institute (2003) *Offshoring: Is it a Win–Win Game?* McKinsey & Company, San Francisco.

Further Reading

Berger, A. (2003) *Smart Things to Know about Six Sigma.* Capstone Publishing, Oxford.

British Computer Society (1993) *The Sourcer's Apprentice: A Guide to IT Sourcing for Decision Makers.* British Computer Society, Swindon.

Burnett, R. (1998) *Outsourcing IT: The Legal Aspects.* Gower Publishing, Aldershot (second edition due for publication early 2005).

Gay, C. L. and Essinger, J. (2000) *Inside Outsourcing: The Insider's Guide to Managing Strategic Sourcing.* Nicholas Brealey, London.

Hirschheim, R., Heinzel, A. and Dibbern, J. (eds) (2002) *Information Systems Outsourcing: Enduring Themes, Emergent Patterns and Future Directions.* Springer-Verlag, Berlin.

Kakabadse, A. and Kakabadse, N. (2002) *Smart Sourcing: International Best Practice.* Palgrave, Basingstoke.

Office of Government Commerce (2002) *IS Management and Business Change Guides: How to Manage Service Acquisition.* Format Publishing, Norwich.

Sparrow, E. (2003) *Successful IT Outsourcing: From Choosing a Provider to Managing the Project.* Springer-Verlag, London.

BCS Products and Services

Other products and services from the British Computer Society, which might be of interest to you include:

Publishing

BCS publications, including books, magazines and peer-review journals, provide readers with informed content on business, management, legal, regulatory and emerging technological issues, supporting the professional, academic and practical needs of the IT community. www.bcs.org/publications.

Qualifications

The BCS Professional Examination is an internationally recognized qualification that provides the underpinning education needed for a career in computing and IT. The final stage is examined to the academic level of an honours degree. www.bcs.org/exam.

Information Systems Examination Board (ISEB) qualifications add value to professional careers by providing both the means and the platform for recognition and enhanced career development. Qualification areas cover Management, Development, Quality and Service Management. www.iseb.org.uk.

European Certification of IT Professionals (EUCIP) is aimed at IT Professionals and Practitioners wishing to gain professional certification and competency development. www.bcs.org/eucip.

European Computer Driving Licence® **(ECDL)** is the internationally recognized computer skills qualification which enables people to demonstrate their competence on computer skills. ECDL is managed in the UK by the BCS. ECDL Advanced has been introduced to take computer skills certification to the next level and teaches extensive knowledge of particular computing tools. www.ecdl.co.uk.

Professional Products

The BCS promotes the use of an industry standard IT skills framework forming the basis of a range of professional development products and services for both individual practitioners and employers. www.bcs.org/products.

Networking and Events

The BCS's national network of branches and specialist groups enables members to exchange ideas and keep abreast of latest developments. www.bcs.org/sg.

The Society's programme of social events, lectures, awards schemes, and competitions provides more opportunities to network. www.bcs.org/events.

Further Information

This information was correct at the time of publication, but could change in the future. For the latest information, please contact: The British Computer Society, 1 Sanford Street, Swindon, Wiltshire, SN1 1HJ. Telephone +44 (0)1793 417 424 E-mail: bcshq@hq.bcs.org.uk Web: www.bcs.org.

To receive information about new BCS books and publications and special offers, join the Books Update email service. www.bcs.org/booksupdate.

Index

access to skills and resources 35–36
acquisitions of offshore service providers 11–12
ADCOS 139
administration aspects of performance management 86–87
advantages and benefits of offshore outsourcing 25, *Table 2.1*
alliances with offshore service providers 11
American Management Systems (AMS) 136–137
Amicus, response to offshore outsourcing trend 15
analysis of IT services, place in sourcing strategy 59–60
application development 34
application environment 64
application life cycle 63
application problems 63–64
audit rights 77
ARoBS Transilvania Software 139
Association for Consulting to Business (Czech Republic) 110
Association of the Brazilian Companies of Software and IT Services (ASSESPRO) website 99
Association of the Computer and Multimedia Industry, Malaysia (PIKOM) 129

Bag Lady, The, website 91–92, 96
Brazil
  background information 97
  company profile 99
  facts and figures 98
  further information 99
  offshore IT services industry 98–99
Brazilian Association of Software Companies (ABES) website 99
Britannia Airways 75–76
British Computer Society, response to offshore outsourcing trend 16–18
Bulgaria
  background information 99–100
  company profile 101
  facts and figures 100
  further information 101
  offshore IT services industry 101
Bulgarian Association of Information Technologies (BAIT) 101

Bulgarian Foreign Investment Agency 101
business case analysis 65–66
business models 6–12
Business Start Page, The, website 92
business transformation 38

Canada
  background information 102
  company profiles 103–104
  facts and figures 102–103
  further information 104
  offshore IT services industry 103
Capability Maturity Model (CMM)
  generally 29–32
  CMMI levels 30–31, *Table 2.2*
  variants on 30
Certified Information System Security Professional (CISSP) examination 48
CGI 103–104
change control 77, 88
China
  background information 104–105
  company profiles 107
  facts and figures 105
  further information 107–108
  offshore IT services industry 105–107
China Offshore Software Engineering Project (COSEP) 106
China Software Industry Association (CSIA) 108
choosing service providers
  due diligence 74–76
  evaluation process
    generally 69–70, *Figure 4.3*
    financial appraisal 72
    project evaluation 71
    supplier assessment 70–71
  selecting preferred bidder 72–74
  short-listing potential suppliers 72
CMMI levels 30–31, *Table 2.2*
Cognizant, development centres in India 32
Cognizant Technology Solutions 118
Colgate 9
Common Criteria (CC) standards in security products 48
communication, importance of 85–86
Computer Sciences Corporation 148
Confederation of British Industry, response to offshore outsourcing trend 20
confidentiality
  of business information 47–49, 63

  of contracts 77
contract management 86–87
contracts, for outsourcing
  award of 82
  confidentiality aspects 77
  data protection issues 77, 79
  due diligence aspects of 75
  generally 76–77
  negotiations 81–82
  service level agreement 79–81
  structure 77–79
  termination provisions 79
core business objectives, focus on 36–37
corporate objectives 58
corporate values 58
cost reduction 25–27
countermeasures to risks of offshore outsourcing 39–55
country profiles
  Brazil 97–99
  Bulgaria 99–101
  Canada 102–104
  China 104–108
  Czech Republic 108–110
  generally 89–91
  Hungary 110–112
  India 112–122
  information resources 91–95
  Ireland 122–124
  Israel 125–127
  key to 96–97
  Malaysia 127–129
  Mexico 129–131
  Philippines, The 131–134
  Poland 135–137
  Romania 137–140
  Russia 140–143
  Singapore 143–146
  South Africa 146–149
  Vietnam 149–151
Country Watch website 92
cultural differences 41–43
customer backlash 52–53
customer references 75
Cyberjaya 129
Czech Republic
  background information 108
  company profile 110
  facts and figures 108–109
  further information 110
  offshore IT services industry 109
CzechInvest 110
CWU, response to offshore outsourcing trend 15

163

data protection
  business information and 47–49
  contracts and 77
Data Protection Act 1998 (UK) 46–47
Dell 50
DHL 110
Dialogue Group 148
difficult business environments 43–44
Digital Philippines Foundation 134
dispute resolution principles, in contracts 78
due diligence
  company 75
  contractual 75
  customer references 75
  generally 74
  price 74
  solution 74–75

easyCinema 26–27
economic advantages of offshore outsourcing 25–28
Economist Intelligence Unit website 92
EDM International 131
EDS Best Shore 7
EIU Viewswire service 96
Eontec 123–124
EPAM 142
evaluation
  of projects 71
  of service providers
    financial appraisal 72
    generally 69–70, *Figure 4.3*
    project evaluation 71
    supplier assessment 70–71
Executive Planet(tm) website 92
extension of working day, as benefit of offshore outsourcing 34–35

financial appraisal of service providers 72
flexibility, loss of 51
Foxtons 36–37

geopolitical instability 43–44
Global CyberSoft 150–151
global delivery models 6, *Table 1.1*
Global InServe model 12
global IT departments 9–10
global organic growth 12
global sourcing
  future of 153–155
  introduction to 1–23
governance structures, and sourcing strategy 62
government responses to offshore outsourcing trend 20–23

hardware requirements 63
Harvey Nash 153
HCL Technologies 118–119
hidden costs 40
Hieros Gamos Employment Law website 92–93
Hong Kong Information Technology Federation (HKITF) 107–108

HSBC 129
Hungarian Association of Information Technology Companies (IVSZ) 112
Hungarian Investment and Trade Development Agency 112
Hungarian Software Alliance (HSA) 112
Hungary
  background information 110–111
  company profile 112
  facts and figures 111
  further information 112
  offshore IT services industry 111–112

iConcepts 101
IDA Ireland 124
India
  background information 112–113
  company profiles 118–121
  facts and figures 113–114
  further information 121–122
  offshore IT services industry 114–118
  success in global sourcing market 153
Indiana Department of Workforce Development 53
Information and Computer Technologies Industry Association (APKIT) website 143
Information Industry South Africa 149
information resources, on country profiles 91–95
Information Technology Association of Canada (ITAC) 104
Information Technology Association of the Philippines (ITAP) 134
Information Technology Landscape in Nations Around the World website 93
Infosys Technologies 32, 119
Intel 126
Intellect
  Offshore Group Code of Practice 19, 157–158
  response to offshore outsourcing trend 17–18
intellectual property protection 45–46
International Growth website 93
International Monetary Fund website 93–94
IPACRI 139
Ireland
  background information 122
  company profiles 123–124
  facts and figures 122–123
  further information 124
  offshore IT services industry 123
Irish Software Association (ISA) 124
ISO 9000 29
Israel
  background information 125
  company profile 126
  facts and figures 125
  further information 126–127

offshore IT services industry 126
Israeli Association of Software Houses (IASH) 126–127
IT services
  analysis of, and sourcing strategy 59–60
  market in, investigation of 68–69
IT strategy, alignment with sourcing strategy 62
i-Vantage 12

joint ventures with offshore service providers 10–11

Keane 104
key performance indicators 87–88
knowledge transfer 63

legal issues 45–46
London Congestion Charging Scheme 21–22
Lonely Planet website 94, 96
LUXOFT 142

Malaysia
  background information 127
  company profile 129
  facts and figures 127–128
  further information 129
  offshore IT services industry 128
management of projects *see performance of projects, managing; projects, managing*
Mastek 22, 119
Metropolitan Police 48–49
Mexican Association of the Information Technology Industry (AMITI) website 131
Mexico
  background information 129–130
  company profile 131
  facts and figures 130
  further information 131
  offshore IT services industry 130–131
Microsoft 107
Ministry of Communications and Information Technology (India) 121
Ministry of Information Industry (MII) (China) 108
Multimedia Development Corporation 129
multinational outsourcing companies 7
multi-sourcing
  advantages and disadvantages of 60–61, *Table 4.1*
  place in sourcing strategy 60–61

National Association of the Software Industry and Services (ANIS) (Romania) 139–140
National Association of Software and Service Companies (NASSCOM) (India) 44, 121
National Health Service 11

National Outsourcing Association, response to offshore outsourcing trend 18–19
National Software Development Alliance 'Silicon Taiga' (Russia) 143
National Software Development Association of Russia (RUSSOFT) 143
NCS 145
near-shore outsourcing, defined 2–3
Nectar loyalty card 37–38
negative impact on IT professionals 53–55
negotiations, for outsourcing contracts 81–82
Neusoft
  joint venture with Philips 10–11
  operations in China 107

object-oriented programming, and offshore outsourcing 3
objectives of projects
  business case analysis 64–65
  generally 64
  risk management 65–66
offshore companies *see offshore service providers*
offshore IT services industry
  Brazil 98–99
  Bulgaria 101
  Canada 103
  China 105–107
  Czech Republic 109
  generally 89–91
  Hungary 111–112
  India 114–118
  Ireland 123
  Israel 126
  Malaysia 128
  Mexico 130–131
  Philippines, The 133
  Poland 136
  Romania 138–139
  Russia 141–142
  Singapore 144–145
  South Africa 147–148
  Vietnam 150
offshore market
  established service providers 8
  growth in 3–4, 4–6
  origins of 4–6
offshore outsourcing
  advantages and benefits of
    access to skills and resources 35–36
    business transformation 38
    core business objectives, focus on 36–37
    cost reduction 25–27
    extension of working day 34–35
    generally 25, *Table 2.1*
    other economic advantages 27–28
    productivity and service improvements 37–38
    quality management 28–33
  contracts for
    award of 82

  confidentiality aspects 77
  data protection issues 77, 79
  due diligence aspects of 75
  generally 76–77
  negotiations 81–82
  service level agreements 79–81
  structure of 77–79
  termination provisions 79
countermeasures in
  confidentiality 47–49
  cultural differences 41–43
  customer backlash 52–53
  data protection 47–49
  difficult business environments 43–44
  generally 39
  geopolitical instability 43–44
  hidden costs 40
  intellectual property protection 45–46
  legal issues 45–46
  loss of flexibility and control 51
  loss of technical expertise 50
  negative impact on IT professionals 53–55
  security 47–49
defining 2–3
economic factors 4
growth in 3–4, 4–6
identifying requirements in 62–64
introduction to 1–23
job reduction caused by 2
nearshore outsourcing compared 2–3
negotiations in 81–82
object-oriented programming and 3
origins of 4–6
process of 58–59, *Figure 4.1*
projects in *see projects*
quality issues 2
questions on 2–4
reasons for using 2
requirements in
  hardware 63
  identifying 62–64
  software 63
  statement of 67–68
  volatile 64
responses to trend in
  generally 13–14
  government 20–23
  professional and trade associations 16–20
  trade unions 14–16
risks of
  confidentiality 46–47
  cultural differences 40–41
  customer backlash 52
  data protection 46–47
  difficult business environments 43
  generally 39, *Table 3.1*
  geopolitical instability 43
  hidden costs 40
  intellectual property protection 44–45
  legal issues 44–45
  loss of flexibility and control 50–51

  loss of technical expertise 49–50
  negative impact on professionals 53–54
  security 46–47
  statement of requirements 67–68
  successful, steps to 58–59, *Figure 4.1*
offshore service providers
  acquisitions of 11–12
  alliances with 11
  emerging 9
  established 8
  joint ventures with 10–11
offshore working, outsourcing companies specializing in 8–9
Organization for Economic Cooperation and Development (OECD) website 94
Outsource Philippines 134
outsourcing companies
  established 7
  multinational 7
  specializing in offshore working 8–9
outsourcing relationships
  developing 84–85
  successful 84, *Figure 4.4*

People CMM (P-CMM) 30
performance of projects, managing
  administration 86–87
  change control 88
  communication 85–86
  contract management 86–87
  developing outsourcing relationships 84–85
  generally 83–84
  key performance indicators 87–88
  resolving problems 88–89
  service management 87–88
Philippines, The
  background information 131–132
  company profiles 133–134
  facts and figures 132–133
  further information 134
  offshore IT services industry 133
Philips, joint venture with Neusoft 10–11
Poland
  background information 135
  company profile 136–137
  facts and figures 135–136
  further information 137
  offshore IT services industry 136
Polish Chamber of Information Technology and Telecommunications (PIIT) 137
Polish Information and Foreign Investment Agency 137
preferred bidder, selecting 72–74
price, due diligence aspects of 74
problems
  applications, in 63–64
  resolving 88–89
process of outsourcing 58–59, *Figure 4.1*
productivity and service improvements, as benefits of offshore outsourcing 37–38

professional and trade associations'
    response to offshore
    outsourcing trend
  British Computer Society 16–18
  Confederation of British Industry 20
  Intellect 19–20
  National Outsourcing Association
    18–19
  Professional Contractors' Group 18
Professional Contractors' Group,
    response to offshore
    outsourcing trend 18
project management *see performance
    of projects, managing; projects,
    managing*
project visibility 63
projects
  evaluation of 71
  managing
    choosing a service provider 69–76
    contracts 76–82
    generally 57–58
    identifying requirements 62–64
    investigating IT services market
      68–69
    objectives 64–67
    performance aspects 83–89
    sourcing strategy 58–62
    statement of requirements 67–68
    transition stage 82–83
  objectives of
    business case analysis 64–65
    generally
    risk management 65–66
  performance of *see performance of
    projects, managing*
  visibility of 63
Prumerica Systems Ireland 124

quality management, as benefit of
    offshore outsourcing
  Capability Maturity Model (CMM)
    29–32, *Table 2.2*
  generally 28–33
  ISO 9000 29
  Six Sigma 33

Request for Proposals (RFP) 72
requirements in offshore outsourcing
  hardware 63
  identifying 62–64
  software 63
  statement of 67–68
  volatile 64
responses to trend in offshore
    outsourcing
  generally 13–14
  government, by 20–23
  professional and trade associations,
    by 16–20
  trade unions, by 14–16
Reuters 28
risk, attitudes to, place in sourcing
    strategy 58
risk management 65–66
risks of offshore outsourcing
  confidentiality 46–47
  cultural differences 40–41

customer backlash 52
data protection 46–47
difficult business environments 43
generally 39, *Figure 3.1*
geopolitical instability 43
hidden costs 40
intellectual property protection
    44–45
legal issues 44–45
loss of flexibility and control 50–51
loss of technical expertise 49–50
negative impact on IT professionals
    53–54
security 46–47
Romania
  background information 137
  company profiles 139
  facts and figures 138
  further information 139–140
  offshore IT services industry
    138–139
Romanian Association for the
    Electronic and Software
    Industry (ARIES) 139
Romanian Association for Information
    Technology and
    Communications (ATIC)
    website 140
Russia
  background information 140
  company profiles 142
  facts and figures 140–141
  further information 142–143
  offshore IT services industry
    141–142

'Safe Harbour' scheme (USA) 47
Safeway 134
Satyam Computer Services 120
SAVANT 148–149
security of business information
    47–49
security products, standards in 48
sensitive data 63
service level agreements
  elements of 79–81
  with suppliers 60–61
service management 87–88
service providers
  see also offshore service providers
  choosing 69–76
  due diligence 74–76
  evaluation process
    financial appraisal 72
    generally 69–70, *Figure 4.3*
    project evaluation 71
    supplier assessment 70–71
  selecting preferred bidder 72–74
  service level agreements with 60–61
  short-listing potential suppliers 72
shared services 10
Shell 10
short-listing potential suppliers 72
Singapore
  background information 143
  company profile 145
  facts and figures 144
  further information 145–146

offshore IT services industry
    144–145
Singapore infocomm Technology
    Federation (SiTF) 145
Singapore Science Park 145–146
single-sourcing, advantages and
    disadvantages of 60–61,
    Table 4.1
Six Sigma 33
Society for IT and
    Telecommunications Users -
    Sao Paolo (Sucesu-SP)
    website 99
Software Acquisition CMM
    (SA-CMM) 30
software requirements 63
Software Technology Parks of India
    (STPI) 121
Software Ventures International
    133–134
Somerfield 35–36
sourcing strategy
  alignment with IT strategy 62
  analysis of IT services and 59–60
  corporate objectives and 58
  corporate values and 58
  elements of 58–62, *Figure 4.2*
  governance structures and 62
  multi-sourcing and 60–61, *Table 4.1*
  risk, attitudes to, and 58
South Africa
  background information 146
  company profiles 148
  facts and figures 146–147
  further information 148–149
  offshore IT services industry
    147–148
staff responses to offshore working 63
statement of requirements 67–68
structure of contracts 77–79
suppliers
  assessment of 70–71
  evaluation process 69–72, *Figure 4.3*
  short-listing potential 72
System Engineering CMM (SE-
    CMM) 30
system integration 63
System Security Engineering CMM
    (SSE-CMM) 30

Tata Consultancy Services 120
team size 63
Team Software Process (TSP) 48
Techlocate website 96
technical expertise, loss of 50
Thames Water 8
TietoEnator 42–43
Trade-related Aspects of Intellectual
    Property rights (Trips) 45
trade unions' response to offshore
    outsourcing trend
  Amicus 15
  CWU 15
  generally 14–15
  Unifi 15–16
Transfer of Undertakings (Protection
    of Employment) Regulations
    (TUPE) (UK) 53–54

Index

transition stage 82–83
Trusted CMM (T-CMM) 30

Unifi, response to offshore outsourcing trend 15–16
user interaction 62

Vetta Technologies 99
Vietnam
  background information 149
  company profiles 150–151
  facts and figures 149–150
  further information 151
  offshore IT services industry 150
Vietnam Software Association (VINASA) 151
virtual helpdesk 34–35, *Table 2.3*
visibility of projects 63
volatile requirements 64

Washington State Health Care Agency 51–52
Wipro, Six Sigma programme at 33
Wipro Technologies 121

work permits 12–13
working day, extension of, as benefit of offshore outsourcing 34–35
World Bank Group: Data and Statistics website 94
World Information Technology and Services Alliance website 94–95
World Intellectual Property Organization (WIPO) website 95
World Trade Organization 45

A Manager's Guide to IT Law

- IT Contracts
- Instructing an IT Consultant
- Intellectual Property Law for Computer Users
- Setting Up Joint Ventures
- Resolving Disputes
- Implementing New Systems
- Avoiding Employment Problems
- Systems Procurement Contracts
- Escrow
- Outsourcing
- Data Protection

Edited by Jeremy Newton & Jeremy Holt
Cover price £25. ISBN: 1-902505-55-7
orders@yps-publishing.co.uk
···▶ www.bcs.org/books/itlaw

THE BRITISH COMPUTER SOCIETY

Business Process Management: A Rigorous Approach

•••▶ *"Martyn Ould has reinvented process modelling for the real world. Throw away pre-conceived ideas of wall-to-wall reengineering charts, workflow diagrams and arcane application logic . . . this important book is essential "*

HOWARD SMITH

The Business Process Management Initiative

Martyn A Ould
ISBN: 1-902505-60-3
Publication date: 2005
orders@yps-publishing.co.uk

•••▶ **www.bcs.org/books/bpm**

Project Management for IT-Related Projects

▶
- Project Planning
- Monitoring & Control
- Change Control
- Estimating
- Risk
- Project Communications
- Quality Control & Assurance

Can You Manage Without it?

Bob Hughes (Editor), Roger Ireland, Brian West,
Norman Smith and David I. Shepherd
ISBN: 1-902505-58-1
Cover price £18
orders@yps-publishing.co.uk

▶ www.bcs.org/books/projectmanagement

BCS
THE BRITISH COMPUTER SOCIETY

Advance your career in IT with...

THE BCS PROFESSIONAL EXAMINATION

- Examined to British Honours Degree level (at Professional Graduate Diploma)
- Internationally recognised
- Study at your own pace
- Direct route to postgraduate study at UK universities
- Entry to Professional membership (MBCS)
- Pathway to Chartered status (CITP)

www.bcs.org/exam/intads

FOR INFORMATION CONTACT CUSTOMER SUPPORT,
THE BRITISH COMPUTER SOCIETY
1 Sanford Street, Swindon SN1 1HJ
Tel: +44 (0)1793 417543
Fax: +44 (0)1793 480270
Email: examenq@hq.bcs.org
quoting reference number 016/0904

THE BRITISH COMPUTER SOCIETY

MTG/PROM/016/0904

SFIA FOUNDATION MEMBER

Business Advantage Through Structured Skills Development

BCS Career*Developer*™

A powerful new web-based solution to help you define, manage and develop the IT skills within your organisation.

- Explore the SFIA*plus* skills framework
- Build a skills inventory
- Generate job descriptions
- Manage project teams
- Identify skills shortages
- Set up personal development cycles

For more details visit:
www.bcs.org/careerdeveloper

Email:
products@hq.bcs.org.uk

or call:
01793 417541

BCS
THE BRITISH COMPUTER SOCIETY

BCS

It's about setting standards Not standing still

There has never been a more rewarding time to join the BCS. We've changed our constitution to become more dynamic. We've streamlined our membership structure to make the benefits of joining more professionally rewarding.

Our position as the industry body for information technology professionals, and the leading chartered engineering institution for IT, has never been stronger. Join today and stand out as a standard-setting professional.

You can find out more, or join straightaway, simply by visiting our website at **www.bcs.org/gofurther**, or by emailing **gofurther@hq.bcs.org.uk** or calling free in the UK on **0800 056 4322** or on **+44 (0)1793 417424**

going further **together**

⊞ BCS

You need to certify the IT skills of your staff...

You need to talk to us

As the Professional Society for the IT industry the British Computer Society has developed a range of certification products to ensure that you and your staff are qualified to use IT. We offer a wide range of qualifications to meet the needs of all organisations and individuals:

EqualSkills	Introduction to computing for absolute beginners
e-Citizen	e-Participation and use of the Internet
ECDL	European Computer Driving Licence – Internationally recognised end-user certification
ECDL Advanced	Power User certification
ISEB	Information Systems Examinations Board – International qualifications for IT practitioners
BCS Professional Exam	Honours Degree level qualification to certify academic and practical skills
EUCIP	European Certification of IT Professionals – Europe wide qualification for IT professionals

To find out more visit our web site: **www.bcs.org/certify**
Or contact us on 01793 417530 or by email: **certify@hq.bcs.org.uk**

   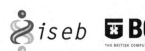